AN AB

C000200017

By the same author

In the Crucible
On the Anvil

AN AFFAIR OF THE HEART

Encountering God in prayer and life

Robert Warren

Highland Books
Guildford, Surrey

Copyright © 1994 Robert Warren.

The right of Robert Warren to be identified as author of
this work has been asserted by him in accordance with the
Copyright, Designs and Patents Act 1988.

British Library Cataloguing-in-Publication Data. A catalogue
record for this book is available from the British Library.

Published by Highland Books, an imprint of Inter Publishing
Service (IPS) Ltd, 59 Woodbridge Road, Guildford, Surrey
GU1 4RF.

All Scripture quotations, unless otherwise noted, are taken from
the New International Version Copyright © 1973, 1978, 1984 by
the International Bible Society. Used by permission of Hodder
Headline.

Typeset by The Electronic Book Factory Ltd, Fife, Scotland.
Printed in the UK by HarperCollins Manufacturing, Glasgow.

ISBN: 1 897913 09 5

Contents

Introduction

*The prayers of the saints
are affairs of the heart*
David Adam, *The Cry of the Deer*, p. 100.

What is an 'officer for evangelism' doing writing a book on prayer? Should he not be 'getting on with the job'?

There are two answers to those questions. The book was written before I took on my present job. It arose out of my desire to help people in today's world, which we will see is hostile to any form of stopping to rediscover prayer. It arose out of a training day for church leaders concerned to help their church members to pray. That has led on to taking this material 'on the road'. It has therefore been tested in action and found to be helpful and workable. The desire to help people pray was further urged forward by the discovery of how few regular worshippers actually prayed. A number of national and local surveys have established that between 60 per cent and 80 per cent of everyone in Britain claims to pray. I sometimes wonder if the rest are the ones who go to church!

However, the more important reason for pressing on with the publication of this book, is the conviction—strengthened since taking on my new role—that prayer and evangelism are inseparable, and that one of the best (and quickest) ways to help forward the work of evangelism is to help people pray. The reason is not difficult to see. Prayer is about our personal experience of God—and evangelism is about telling others of our personal experience of God. The one leads to the other. Moreover, without the one (prayer), the other (evangelism) will always be stunted, artificial and a chore. If married they are likely to have many children. As John Talbot, founder of the Brothers and Sisters of Charity, has put it:

> We cannot evangelise until we have been evangelised. This happens most powerfully through solitary prayer.
> (John Michael Talbot, *Blessings [reflections on the Beatitudes]* p. 16)

This link between prayer ('spirituality') and evangelism is something which Springboard, the Archbishops' initiative in evangelism, has picked up and emphasised in seeing that evangelism—for greatest effectiveness—must function in a threefold cord of evangelism-spirituality-apologetics. All of which leads me to issue the first 'government health warning' about going deeper into prayer—it can seriously affect how you see life, what you talk about, and how you handle your relationships with other people. More of that in due course.

Context

It is important to set prayer in the context of our present culture, for if we do not understand our setting in history we are unlikely to break through to authentic prayer. Here I want to draw attention to some aspects of modern culture which make prayer more difficult.

The pace of life is prayer-resistant. In my previous work as the Team Rector of a flourishing church I used to say that I wondered if the attractiveness of the church was that it was 'a frantic church in a frantic society'. Newcomers felt at home! I then went on to say that God might just want the church to become 'a still church in a frantic society'. Prayer and stillness are certainly close cousins. They have not been seeing much of each other recently.

Our way of communicating is prayer-resistant. By this I mean that we live in a culture which has been deeply shaped by rational, scientific thinking and by cerebral, verbal communication as *the* means of communication. We tend to restrict prayer to 'words said': but prayer is much richer than that, as C.S. Lewis says:

> I still think the prayer without words is the best—if one can really achieve it.
> (C.S. Lewis, *Prayer: Letters to Malcolm*, p. 12)

However, this culture is changing rapidly, from a word-conscious to an image-conscious one. 'Sound-bites' and 'photo-opportunities' now largely shape political communication, as the use of images largely shape advertising. Advertisements tells us little about the product but transport us into an idyllic setting that is meant to leave an association with the wonders of the car/perfume/chocolate/loo fluid being promoted.

My intention in what follows is to open up some of the other, and arguably richer, avenues of prayer. We have much to learn from the Church, down the whole history of Christendom, which could well help us make connection with God in the new culture into which we are moving.

Our way of reading is prayer-resistant. The way we think and communicate in our culture means that we easily end up reading scripture like the handbook for operating a microwave oven, in a literal mechanical way. If you read the Psalms or parables of Jesus like that they will seem dull indeed, and of little or no aid to engaging in prayer. Reading scripture is much more than 'finding out the facts'.

Moreover, such a way of seeing reality misses out the great areas of prayer that have enriched Christian prayer for two millennia, namely symbols, stories, rituals, and a sense of awe and wonder. By exploring them, I hope also to help liberate us a little from the constraints upon the whole of life imposed by the narrowness of our Western way of seeing and living life.

If, in the process of growing in our experience and expression of prayer, we could break through some of these constraints, it might have a significant effect on the work of evangelism. For we would be evangelising our way of seeing life and reality. It was the medieval mystics who said that evangelism is sharing the fruits of our contemplation with others. Much of the teaching of Jesus seems to have that source, for he was sharing the fruit of his meditation on scripture

('You have heard it said . . .'), and on the world around him (hence, the parables).

Not so much a book, more a way of doing prayer

Having introduced myself, and set the work of renewing personal prayer in the wider context of the culture in which we are living, I want to explain my purpose in writing.

Interesting and often helpful though books about prayer are, this book is focused specifically on helping in the *practice* of prayer. It is more of a prayer manual than a discussion about prayer. It arises out of my conviction that much of the seeming impotence of the Church in the West can be traced back to the lack of reality in our engaging with God at the personal level. Talking *about* is no substitute for talking *to* God.

It is for this reason that the book is written with several ingredients in it. First, there is the actual *text* of the book itself in which I spell out various aspects of prayer. Second, in each chapter there is a prayer *exercise* which relates to the material of the chapter. It is intended to be used repeatedly until it becomes part of our way of praying. More about that in a moment. Third, is a series of prayer *principles* scattered throughout the book, and appropriately highlighted in the text. These are principles, which if we can get hold of, and learn to practise, will lay a foundation on which a stronger prayer life can be built. Fourth, scattered through the book are a number of 'Prayers of the heart'. These are prayers which express some major aspect of the life of prayer, and which are best learned by heart. They will then arise out of our inner being wherever we are, including times of sickness and when our eye-sight or other faculties have departed before us, to enrich our closing years of discipleship. These various aspects are all part of the goal of going beyond this being 'another book about prayer', into being a book that is prayer-productive. The aim is to stimulate and guide the practice of prayer.

Which leads me to conclude this introduction with some suggestions about how to make the most of what follows.

Practice

My encouragement is to *pray along with this book* and not just to read it. It may be worth reading through the book first to get the overall feel and direction, but then, its primary value will be in assisting the work and practice of praying.

Here there is a paradox at the heart of learning to pray. It is this, that whilst we can learn much from various 'schools of prayer' and from 'spiritual directors', it is also true that the only way you can pray is the way that *you* can pray. Prayer is unique to each individual. I have no desire therefore, to impose a foreign way of praying on others. Yet, each of us can benefit from being stretched to pray beyond the confines of our present patterns. However, the long-term purpose of being stretched to pray in new ways, is that they will become natural to our way of praying. So all that is presented here needs to be integrated into the way of praying that is authentic to each individual.

PRAYER PRINCIPLE ONE
PRACTICE MAKES PERFECT
*Learning new skills in prayer is always initially
self-conscious;
we have to press through this stage to reach
the productive stage beyond.*

Developing our prayer life is rather like learning
to drive a car. Initially it is all so slow and self-
conscious. Is the seat in the right place? Can I see
out of the mirrors? Where does the ignition key go?
Is the car in gear? Where is the hand-brake, and is
it on? All these questions crowd into the mind of
the learner—even before the engine is switched
on. For the experienced driver, they are well on
their journey before they have given so much conscious thought to the work of driving. They have
assimilated the practice into unconscious skills.

*Accept that learning new skills in prayer is
always self-conscious—but only in the learning
stage.* My encouragement is to press on through
the seeming 'artificiality' of new skills to the place
where we have assimilated them, and found them
enriching our practice of prayer. C.S. Lewis says:

> As long as you notice, and have to count,
> the steps, you are not yet dancing but only
> learning to dance.
> (C.S. Lewis, *Prayer: Letters to Malcolm*, p.6)

The important point is not to be put off by that
self-consciousness, but to press on through it to
the place where 'it works' and 'I can do it' describe
your experience. Without this willingness to press
on through the newness we will not develop new
skills.

Like learning to drive a car, or dance, it is also best to *tackle one aspect at a time*. My encouragement to those wanting to stretch their prayer muscles is to work on one aspect at a time. It may be listening prayer, or beholding the throne, or practising the presence of God that we feel the desire or need to develop. In which case, read the relevant chapter, do the exercise provided, and stay with that for a month or more. As you do this you will assimilate new skills and incorporate them into your own prayer life. The more you practise, the more you will find *your* way of praying taking shape.

Establishing a regular time of prayer or a regular time to work on the exercises in this book, is an important part of preparing to pray. I have found it helpful to agree with myself that to allocate a manageable amount and frequency of prayer is much better than laying unrealistic and discouraging expectations on myself. Better to decide on three sessions of ten minutes of actual prayer, three times a week, and achieve that, than attempt an hour a day and fail gloriously. Once you have achieved your target you can stretch it.

If you are committing yourself to prayer, and working through this book, then it is more a matter of committing yourself to twenty minutes to read a chapter and ten minutes to do the prayer exercise at the end, once a week, and then to repeat the exercise for the next few days/weeks until you are familiar with it and have incorporated it into your prayer life.

If you start with the book and the exercises, do not be put off by feelings of self-consciousness and artificiality. As time, and you, progress, those feelings will fade and a growing sense of this way of praying being natural to you will begin, like crocuses in spring, to show themselves as signs of hope and experiences of joy.

For some, this book may be of most help, if having read it through, you then use the 'Prayer Principles' scattered through the text as an aid to the strengthening of your prayer life. You are likely to find that a number have already been established, and others not. Simply by seeing them in the specific terms in which they are set out can strengthen your already existing practise of them.

Developing your own prayer book

Keeping a journal is a helpful way to grow in prayer. (There is more about the practice of doing this in the Postcript.) Use it to record prayers that arise out of your growth in prayer. You can put quotations, pictures and prayers down for future and repeated reference. Most important, you can record the story of your journey in prayer. The important thing is to 'tell it the way it is'. As you look over it from time to time it will help you to understand the journey you have made so far, and so give understanding of what the next steps need to be.

I also find it a great help to record the prayers (of others, and those that arise spontaneously out of my own experience) which particularly resonate with my experience of life.

That word 'resonate' has a historical context for me. I was taking a wedding in a church with eight chancel steps. I was at the top of them, the bride and groom were one step below and—as I took the

ring from the best man—I noticed that there was a
heating grille running along the base of the bottom
step. The moment of fear ('will I drop the ring?')
was followed by a matching action—I dropped it!
'Ping, ping, ping' it went as it hit the top step and
bounced up again three times. Suddenly out of my
subconscious leapt the awareness that I used to be
a good wicket-keeper at school—especially when
the ball kept low. In an instant I bent my knees,
scooped the ring up at ankle height, and recovered
the situation.

However, I knew that everybody was aware of
what had happened. That tiny ring had hit just the
note to resonate around the whole church. It might
have been Big Ben striking for all the attention it
drew to itself. It is etched deeply into my understanding of the fact that 'to resonate' means 'to
give characteristic vibrations in sympathy with
another body'. It has become an important word
for me in prayer. There are some prayers that
'fill with vibrations' and find a deep echo with
me. Those are the prayers I record, and use again
and again. They attune me to the presence of the
Divine.

The spiritual exercises of Robert Warren

I have to admit that the phrase heading this
section does not have about it quite the ring of
the phrase from which it is taken, namely *The
Spiritual Exercises of Ignatius of Loyola*! However, I dare to use the phrase because the book
really is a book of spiritual or prayer exercises,
and I find the whole idea of exercise fits well with
my understanding and experience of prayer.

We take exercise, or do exercises, for our own health and well-being. So too with prayer. It does demand effort, but the experts tell us not to 'over-stretch' ourselves. So too with prayer. We have to learn new exercises and then we can become proficient in their practice and grow in what we can do through them. So too with prayer. A regular ten or so minutes is much better than a marathon every decade. So too with prayer.

In particular, a schedule of exercises is designed to use, develop and bring to fitness, our whole body. So there will be neck and shoulder exercises, and upper body exercises, and chest exercises and leg and arm exercises, and so on. So too with prayer. This is a major part of this book. The different parts of the body, as far as prayer is concerned, include the use of the body itself (how we sit and how we breathe), the use of the eyes (with the use of pictures of places and people that have 'spoken to us' and of icons), the use of our imagination (either in reading scripture or in a 'prayer visitation', or of a trouble-spot in the News), and the development of our capacity for wonder, awe, and stillness. The aim of this book is to help us develop our prayer muscles. It is a form of spiritual aerobics, although definitely not narrowly spiritual as an important concern is to connect the inner spiritual life with our outer experience of reality.

On fire

Picking up and reading this book is an indication of the desire to grow in the glorious skill and gift of prayer. My prayer is that those who see it through to the end may find it to be an enriching experience that is life-giving not just to our prayer life, but rather to the whole of life. As Jesus so clearly demonstrated in his person, to pray is to live, and to grow in prayer is to grow in the capacity to enjoy life.

PRAYER OF THE HEART:
Caim for stilling our hearts
(a 'caim' is a Celtic 'circle prayer').

Encircle me O God
  keep faith within
  keep pride without

Encircle me O God
  keep hope within
  keep despair out

Encircle me O God
  keep love within
  keep fear without
                    (Adapted from David Adam's
                    The Cry of the Deer, p. 11ff.)

Roberta Bondi, in her fine book *To Pray and to Love (Conversations on Prayer with the Desert Fathers)*, quotes this wonderful story from one of the Desert Fathers:

Abba Lot went to see Abba Joseph and said to him, 'Abba, as far as I can, I say my little office, I fast a little, I pray and meditate, I live in peace and as far as I can, I purify my thoughts. What else can I do?' Then the old man stood up and stretched his hands toward heaven. His fingers became like ten lamps of fire and he said to him, 'If you will, you can become all flame.'

Prayer exercise: in company with the Three Graces

Sit down, still yourself from the busyness around you, from which you have come, and relax your limbs. Say the prayer (from the hymn 'Come, Holy Spirit, ever One', which can be found on p. 46 of *Celebrating Common Prayer*):

> Love light up our mortal frame,
> Till others catch the living flame.

Say it half a dozen to a dozen times, until you do not have to look at the words on the page. Slow down the pace of your saying it each time you repeat it, until the saying of it itself is part of the relaxing process.

Then say it 'in the company of the three graces', namely Faith, Hope and Love, repeating it in the awareness of each of these graces in turn.

Say it with Faith (repeating it several times), looking to God and expecting him to bring fulfilment of this godly desire to birth in your life.

Say it with Hope, looking to what your prayer life can become. Let Hope open your eyes to the sort of person you can be as the result of being shaped by prayer. See the words of this prayer coming to life in your life. See yourself enlarged in your openness to the whole of life, and more comfortable with living as a creature before the Creator, ignited by love of God and love from God.

Say it with Love, receiving Love as a gift—not straining after it as achievement or making it 'another thing I ought to do'. Know that through prayer you are connected to the source of Love. Do not depend on feelings. They come and go. God's love abides, beneath the changing waters of life, his depths are underneath the often choppy seas of life.

PART ONE

ENCOUNTER

Chapter 1

On the Threshold
Clearing the Obstacles to Prayer

I am a firm believer in regular devotions,
In fact I study my Bible almost every day of
the week.
Almost on Monday, almost on Tuesday,
almost on ...
(*Church of England Newspaper* cartoon)

Our cat, a half Siamese, black creature whose mother had a long pedigree but no morals, and whose father was never seen again, is put out each evening. My locking-up routine involves letting him back in. Frequently, when I open the front door, I find him sitting on the mat outside. He has developed a range of responses. Sometimes he continues to look straight ahead without even an acknowledgement that the door has opened or that the master of the house has called. Sometimes he does look round, but not for long. On occasions I step down to pick him up only to have him shoot away into the night not to be seen until the next morning. And, just sometimes, he gets up, turns round and walks into the house as if this were his invariable practice.

Christians are like that when it comes to prayer. We have been invited into the presence of God ('to dwell in the house of the Lord for ever' Ps 23:6), but we can stand unsure on the threshold. We know the way is open, but we sometimes feel too unsure even to dare to notice. At other times we know prayer is an option but do not avail ourselves of this invitation. Too often, we run and hide ourselves in activity. Yet just sometimes we seem able to walk into God's presence as if this were the most natural thing in the world.

The most natural thing in the world

At one level prayer is that. Opinion polls show that most people in the United Kingdom pray. The human heart is built like that. As St Augustine put it, 'Our hearts are restless until they find their rest in Thee'. The Christian understanding of this human instinct is that we are made to be worshipping creatures. We all instinctively focus our living around some 'centre'. 'She lived for her family', 'he lived for his work', are phrases one hears so often at funerals. It tells you where the centre of a person's life is, or was.

We recognise more easily the false worship, the idols, of those addicted to drugs or alcohol or the pursuit of money, but anything that takes the ultimate focus off God in a person's life is an idol, irrespective of whether it is a 'good thing' like the family, or 'bad thing' like drugs. The point to grasp here is that all these centres are ways of worship—manifestations of the human hunger for connectedness with Ultimate Reality, for a sense of the Transcendence, for what Rudolf Otto called the 'Holy Other'.

This touches on the paradox of human existence. We hunger and long for relationship with God—and yet we will do anything to avoid it. So, if we are to make progress in prayer, we need to see not only that it is a very natural and human response to life, but also something that we instinctively avoid.

Progress will therefore involve the removal of the obstacles. For the fact is that our normal experience is that prayer is a struggle, and often leaves us feeling that, whatever our gift may be, it is not being a gifted pray-er. Why is there this strange ambivalence and evident uncertainty as to whether we want to pray or not? We are like the proverbial hedgehogs wanting to keep warm in winter but unsure as to whether the pain of closeness is not greater than the warmth generated.

PRAYER OF THE HEART:
Collect for purity (to be prayed with awareness of good, God-given, desires).

Almighty God,
to whom all hearts are open,
all desires known,
and from whom no secrets are hidden:
cleanse the thoughts of our hearts
by the inspiration of your Holy Spirit,
that we may perfectly love you,
and worthily magnify your holy name;
through Christ our Lord. Amen.

ASB, p. 119

It was Henry Ford who said that 'thinking is
such hard work, which is why so few people engage
in it.' Perhaps he had not tried prayer, which is
even more demanding. Or so it seems.

Obstacles to prayer

If we are to stand any chance of entering in
through the door that has been opened for us, we
are going to have to leave behind these hindrances,
for they block our way in. Or rather, the blockages
within us make our response to the invitation
so varied and seemingly unpredictable that we
struggle to make progress.

William Cowper, the hymn writer, expressed
the feelings of many of us when he wrote:

> What various hindrances we meet,
>   in coming to the mercy seat!
> Yet who that knows the worth of prayer
>   but wishes to be often there?

Or did he overstate the case? Do we wish to be
'often there'? If we do, we also have to admit
that the wish does not seem to be father to the
deed. Our wishes are impotent. So let us look
at the obstacles and see if we can clear them
out of our way. There are three that stand out,
in my experience and from my listening to the
experience of others.

Allergy

We had better start with the most threatening
obstacle—sin. It is our distance from God in

character and moral judgement, in wisdom and courage, which keeps us at arm's length. We are like Adam hiding in the garden (of activity).

Our problem is compounded by poor diagnosis. All too often today, we see sin in a shallow way. Certainly if you have just sworn at your boss or spouse it makes you feel unworthy to pray. But surface actions are not the real problems. The obstacle is deeper than that. The real killers of the prayer life are pride and unbelief, for pride says 'Leave this to me, God, I can handle it', and unbelief says 'If I don't do something no one (not even God) will', Not that we often say these words, even to ourselves. Yet they lie at the base of much of our attitude towards life and God. Indeed, a major part of the problem is that we deny the truth, and so cannot find healing. There is no one so difficult to cure as the person who thinks they are fit. That is the deep-seated and corrosive nature of sin. Richard Lovelace defines sin as:

> an organic network of compulsive attitudes, beliefs and behaviour, deeply rooted in our alienation from God.
> (Richard Lovelace, *Dynamics of Spiritual Life* [Paternoster Press, Exeter. '79] p. 88)

The problem is that deep. The Puritans were right, mankind does have an allergy to God. The apostle Paul, in his reflections on the state of human nature, concludes that sin is essentially hatred towards God—'the sinful mind is hostile to God' (Rom 8:7).

Irena Ratushinskaya, the Russian poet imprisoned under the communist regime simply for writing poems about God, spoke about her experience at the C.S. Lewis Oxford Institute, in 1992. She said she had come to the conclusion that the former Soviet Union was not, as it claimed, an atheistic state. It was not atheistic, that is not believing in God, but one that believed in God but was motivated by a deep hatred towards him. An anti-God crusade, she said, lay close to the heart of the orientation of the whole structure of government and education. Indeed she said she came to faith because, with everyone and the whole system against him, she thought it was rather unfair and someone ought to be on his side!

One of the clearest evidences of this pride and unbelief is evident in the way that we approach prayer. We see it as something that we do, or are quite capable of doing. We may complain that God does not always turn up, but we actually feel (though rarely admit) that lack of success in prayer is not for want of *our* trying.

Our allergy to God is real. The good news is that help is at hand. For the truth of the matter is that prayer is beyond us. It can only be done by the grace of God: but by the grace of God *it can be done*. That is something which God is always ready to do. The problem is at our end. Paul grasped this truth when he said, 'We do not know what we ought to pray for, but the Spirit himself intercedes for us with groans that words cannot express' (Rom 8:26). The disciples were similarly aware of their inability to pray and were provoked by the poverty of their prayer life compared with what they had seen of the prayer life of Jesus, so they dared to say 'Lord teach us to pray' (Lk 11:1).

The first beatitude is glorious good news about our allergy if we could but grasp it:

Blessed are the poor in spirit, for theirs is the kingdom of heaven. (Matt 5:3)

The reason that this is such good news is that it is an invitation to us to own our weakness and look to God for help. Once we do that we have begun to engage in true prayer, which is a divinely energised way of communication between frail creature and merciful Creator. All we have to do is own the fact that prayer is not something we can do on our own. Then, in that very act we begin to pray. For the grace—sheer undeserved gift—is the basis of prayer just as it is the basis of all creation, including the gift of life itself. And it is grace which lays the axe to the root of pride and unbelief. If we simply admit that we cannot pray, but that God—by his Spirit—can enable us to pray, then we can build a prayer life on the only sure foundation there is; God's generosity to his whole creation.

Too easily today we come to prayer as if all we needed was a little more information, and a little more effort, and the job would be done. The sober truth is that, as the Anglican Prayer Book puts it 'without You we are not to please You'.

What we need is the same attitude as that of the church in the early centuries of Christian discipleship. Then, when someone professed faith, the first thing the church did was to administer exorcism. By this act the church was dealing with the fact that 'the god of this age has blinded the minds of unbelievers' (2 Cor 4:4). So, too, we need to lay aside our pretensions to be able to pray,

and then ask God for his help. It will open the
door to prayer—prayer on the proper basis of a
relationship with God sustained by God himself.

Frailty

Having addressed the major obstacle to our praying, namely the deep-seated allergy to God in the
human heart, we can turn now to the matter which
often engages our attention, namely the feeling
that 'I don't know what to do'. We feel the need
for practical help. That, of course, is a great step
to take for it is a recognition of our creatureliness
and our need of help. It makes us open to help
from others.

God alone can deal with our allergy, but the
saints around us and who have gone before us
can give us much help and encouragement with
our frailty. However, as I have already said, 'you
can only pray in the way that *you* can pray'. In
other words there is a unique way of praying for
every believer—rather like our fingerprints, it is
part of our uniqueness before God.

My intention, therefore, in all that follows, is
so to draw on the resources of the 'saints' that
we can make it our own and incorporate insights
into our own way of praying. This takes time, and
it is important that not too much is attempted at
any one time. I suspect that working through the
exercises (for example, one a month) until we have
made them all our own, is the work of two or three
years. This book is really a 'prayer companion',
something to have alongside you where you pray
so that you can dip into it for new resources for
your prayer life from time to time.

Prayer is like a journey, and I neither want

to lay down tramlines which entirely dictate the how, when and where of that journey, nor simply describe the beautiful sunset that appears on the distant horizon but leave the reader with no help in getting there. The writers of the Book of Common Prayer expressed the same concern in the marvellous language of their day when they wrote:

> It hath been the wisdom of the Church of England, ever since the first compiling of her Publick Liturgy, to keep the mean between the two extremes, of too much stiffness in refusing, and too much easiness in admitting any variation from it.
> (The Preface, *The Book of Common Prayer*, opening sentence.)

What follows is more like giving a map, a compass and some basic instructions about how to make the best use of them. They are given so that you may make your journey. Or to change the metaphor, I have supplied some ingredients for the prayer life, plus a recipe, but you may have to vary the ingredients according to what is available, and the means of cooking, in order for you to make the cake that you are best able to make.

Folly

The third obstacle to prayer is our sheer folly. Here is the greatest gift known to humanity—the privilege of communing with the God who created us and all that is—and yet we neglect this pearl of great price, which is the gift of the gospel.

As a clergyman, I acknowledge that this is one

of the great ironies of our life. We know, and spend most of our waking hours teaching others, how the heart of the good news is that each one of us can know the living God; yet we take so little time to avail ourselves of this gift and privilege.

I had a sobering experience of this whilst leading a team of five clergy and one layman in my former parish. We had identified some major problem in the life of the church and, as chairman of the team, I had asked 'What shall we do about this?' All five clergyman were about to open their mouths to give the group the benefit of their insights when the layman cut the conversation short by saying 'Pray, you dumbos!' It was a timely reminder of our instinct to manage by ourselves, and only turn to God as a last resort—yet we had all preached against such attitudes. How right Rudolf Bultmann, the celebrated German theologian, was when he defined sin in these terms:

> Sin is man's determination to manage by himself.

This folly of not availing ourselves of the greatest privilege of the Christian faith, is nothing new. Bernard of Clairvaux, one of the greatest leaders of the Benedictine order of monks, writing in the twelfth century, saw this same folly in his day. He expresses his dismay in his exposition of the opening words of the Song of Songs, 'Let him kiss me with the kisses of his mouth'. Bernard begins his commentary with these words:

> During my frequent pondering on the burning desire with which the patriarchs longed

for the incarnation of Christ, I am stung by
sorrow and shame. Even now I can scarcely
restrain my tears, so filled with shame am I
by the lukewarmness, the frigid unconcern of
these miserable times. For which of us does
the consummation of that event fill with as
much joy as the mere promise of it inflamed
the desires of the holy men of pre-Christian
times.

Preparing the Way

There is a danger in beginning a book on prayer by
writing about the obstacles. Those who pick up the
book looking for help might well feel discouraged
and confirmed in their sense of failure. However,
the reason for doing so is positive in intention.
Obstacles to prayer act like a ball and chain
around the ankle of the runner-after-prayer. The
best way to make progress is to admit that they
are there and to take them off.

The work of this chapter has been like the task
of the Voice in the Wilderness as recorded in Isaiah
who called:

In the desert prepare
    the way for the Lord;
make straight in the wilderness
    a highway for our God.
Every valley shall be raised up,
    every mountain and hill made low;
the rough ground shall become level,
    the rugged places a plain.

And the glory of the Lord will be revealed,
 and all mankind together will see it.
For the mouth of the Lord has spoken.
                                  (Is 40:3–5)

Our prayer life often seems like a desert and a
wilderness. The promise is that right there is
where God can build a way into his presence. In
fact, the Voice sees the preparation as making us
ready for his coming. He is the one who will 'visit'
us with his salvation and presence. Our task is to
make 'a way'.

We can do that as we remove the high places—
the mountains and hills. There are two that come
to mind. First is the allergy which reveals the
pride of our independence from God. We remove
that simply by owning it and giving it to God
for him to incinerate; that is what confession is.
Second is the other sense in which 'high places'
is used in scripture. It is those places where
other gods hold sway and idols are worshipped.
We will look at that in more detail in Chapter Six
(entitled 'Good Grief!'). However, this is the good
news about repentance, once we have the courage
to own something as our responsibility we are able
to give it away in confession to God. It is what we
deny is ours that 'clings so closely'. The allergy of
pride can be named for what it is and dealt with
swiftly in that way. The very act opens us up to
God and his coming in grace.

Frailty and folly are more like the valleys—the
gaps which need to be filled in. They are more
easily dealt with. Frailty can be levelled by learning from others, folly by seeing our prayerlessness
as such. Moreover, when we see answers to our
frailty, in the form of some accessible 'how to pray'

helps, we can then step out of our folly and enter
into prayer.

So now we can turn our attention to entering
into prayer as we consider an overall framework
which describes both how we meet God in the
whole of life, and how we meet him in prayer.

PRAYER EXERCISE: Letting go and receiving, before God

Sit down in a relaxed manner, resting your hands
on your upper thighs, with your palms facing
down.

Letting go
See your 'hands down' as expressing a letting go
of anything that blocks your awareness of God.
Remember that 'underneath are the everlasting
arms' (Deut 33:27 RSV)
– you are not 'letting go' into a dark abyss but into
  the hands of the God who sustains you
– you will often find that, at the right time, the
  matters you let go will pop back into your mind,
– complete with an answer, a solution, a way
  forward, a new perspective on it, attached.
God is creative and productive in his taking care
of us. We can let go, safely.

Name your excuses for not praying.
Feel your fears of God/prayer/failure.
Picture your allergies, frailty and folly.
letting them go: imagining them dropping out
    of your hands, off your finger tips.

(You may find it helpful to think of them like
stones dropped in a pond: you see the splash each

time and you know it has gone. You may be able
to feel the relief and freedom.)

Taking hold
Turn your hands upwards, still resting them on
your thighs
– keeping them open as an expression of receiving.
Thank God for the gift of his presence, imagine
him placing gifts physically in your hands.

   Give thanks for the gift of prayer.
   Receive his friendship and presence.
   Take hold of the gifts of peace, and hope
      and joy.
   See and feel your sufficiency in Christ for the
      work of prayer.

'You have been given fulness in Christ' (Col
2:10).
(You may find it helpful to see those gifts as water
poured out
– a symbol of life-giving refreshment
– as well as symbolic of the water of baptism which
  marks us as belonging to Christ.)

Be still
Stay in God's presence and enjoy the peace, still-
ness and security that are found in him.
(You may 'feel' nothing: faith enables us to trust
that we already have these gifts.)
Get used to simply being in God's presence—and
not having to fill the time with words.
You may find it helps to say just the three words:
'Our Father in heaven',
– slowly and repeatedly. Enjoy his presence.

The story is told of an elderly woman, confined to bed, who always had a rosary in her hands, but never 'used it': that is, her hands never moved beyond the first bead. Someone berated her one day for 'never using her rosary'. The elderly woman later shared with a friend: 'I never get past those first two words, "Our Father", I just hold them in my heart. I never feel like going on.' (Quoted by Leonard Foley in *Slowing down the Our Father*, St Anthony's Press, USA. '86 p. 7.)

Chapter 2

An Open Door
Prayer as Encounter

*The great fact for which all religion stands
is the confrontation of the human soul
with the transcendent holiness of God.*
John Baillie, *Our Knowledge of God.* p. 3

*Formal moments of prayer are intensified
encounters within a continuous process
of awareness.*
Jack Dominian, *Cycles of Affirmation* (Darton,
Longman and Todd. London. '75) p. 121

Pray as you can, not as you can't
anon

Three themes weave themselves through the pages of scripture like the threefold cord of Ecclesiastes, which we are told 'is not quickly broken' (Eccl 4:12). They are story, journey and encounter.

Story

Scripture is full of story. It is the story of God's existence, of his creation of all that is, and of

his revelation to humanity. It is the story of his
people, and their experience of God. More than
this, it is the story of God's visitation by word, by
the Word-made-flesh and the Holy Spirit, with a
view to bringing 'all things in heaven and on earth
together under one head, even Christ' (Eph 1:10)
In short, scripture can be described as 'a brief
history of eternity'.

It is in this story that we find our story, in which
our identity is bound up. For each of us has a story.
When we say to someone 'tell me about yourself',
they usually tell us their story. The healing power
of scripture is that it gives a context, a setting, and
also a yardstick by which to measure and interpret
our story.

Indeed, baptism is baptism into his story, the
story of Jesus. We enter his death and resurrection, are filled with his Spirit, and 'follow in his
footsteps'. As we do so we experience Cross-and-
Resurrection as a way of life. The pain of broken
relationships, and the joy of their restoration; the
pain of dashed hopes, and the healing power of
new beginnings. The pain of injustice, wounds
and abuse, and the transforming impact of our
acceptance 'in the Beloved'. His story is repeated
in the life of the believer.

Journey

The stories which fill the scriptures, and give
meaning and revelation to our stories, are essentially stories of journey—epic journeys.

The first, and saddest one, is Adam and Eve's
journey out of paradise and into darkness. But
it is quickly followed by stories filled with hope.
The courage of Abraham who 'went, even though

he did not know where he was going' (Heb 11:8),
the pain—yet ultimate triumph—of Joseph on his
dark journey into Egypt and his 'resurrection'
to new life in that strange new world. These
patriarchal journeys are followed by *the* epic journey of the children of Israel as they made *exodus*
(literally 'exit'), out of the bondage of Egypt, to
the mount of revelation at Sinai, and on into the
promised land; where they become established in
their space, and become a new people.

The theme of journey continues into exile in
Babylon, and back again in a new exodus (the
return from exile) under Ezra and Nehemiah, and
the spiritual journey into a new understanding
of holiness and justice as revealed through the
prophets.

The New Testament sustains this theme, setting the ministry of Jesus in the context of journey
to which the disciples are called to 'follow me'.
Many of his greatest stories are stories of epic
journeys. The story of the good Samaritan, and
of the prodigal son, are two such journeys which
resulted in a different person arriving at the des-
tination from the one who set out.

The heart and climax of the story of Jesus is,
of course, the story of a journey. The journey
to Jerusalem, and Jesus going 'the way of the
cross', to Calvary. The risen Lord appearing to
the disciples on the road to Emmaus continues
into the resurrection era the sense of journey. So
in the Acts of the Apostles, it is not surprising to
discover that the early description of discipleship
is called simply 'the Way'.

We too are on a journey through life. Again,
when we want to get to know another person we
ask 'where do you come from?' Our journey gives

us our identity. Which is why, for example, children who have been adopted, have a deep longing to find out about their natural parents—and are often eager to meet them. Knowing where I come from tells me who I am.

I love the story of the young mother who, on collecting her six-year-old daughter from school in the car one day, was suddenly posed with the question that parents dread being asked, (simply because they do not know how to express the answer) namely 'Mummy, where did I come from?' So, taking a deep breath, as she wove the car in and out of the rush hour traffic across town, she gave as coherent and simple an explanation of the intricacies and delicacies of the human reproductive system as she could. When she reached the end she felt herself settling back in her seat with a sigh of relief and some considerable sense of satisfaction at a job well done. It was not destined to last long, for the voice from the back of the car said, in a dismissive tone of voice, 'Yes, Mummy, I know all about that—but I want to know where I came from. Amanda came from Bath, and Jane from Liverpool, where did I come from?'! Knowing where we come from says much about who we are. It gives us our identity.

It is for this reason that 'testimony' plays an important part, not just in Christian witness, but in Christian identity. Telling 'how we got here' says much about our understanding of who we are. Indeed, in my recent work I have been looking at what makes churches become life-giving, serving, outward-going communities of faith. One of the books that has helped me most in this work is James Hopewell's book called, simply, *Congregation*. His central thesis is that you can

only understand a community of believers, and
help to bring about change, if you understand the
story of their journey—as you listen to their history. In other words, what is true for the individual
is true for a community. The story of their journey
of faith tells you who and what they are.

Encounters

What makes stories and journeys so interesting
and varied are the encounters which take place
on the way. They often take place at a cross-
road; seemingly chance encounters have a habit of
changing the direction in which people are going.
That is essentially the nature of a Christian testimony, they are stories of encounters with God—on
the way that led to the Way.

Scripture is full of such encounters.

Jacob wrestles with the angel until he obtains a
blessing. It happens on a journey; a journey down
memory lane—painful memory lane, as he returns
home to put his relationship right with the brother
he cheated. A fighter by nature (in the womb and
in life), he 'takes on the angel' and is wounded in
the thigh. But the wound brings healing, it touches
him with his creatureliness, his limits, his need of
God's blessing and direction. It is an encounter
which changes who he is, and the course of his
life. It is one of the few encounters in scripture
which takes place in the dark. Yet often, as we
shall see in Chapter Six, that is just where we
encounter God.

Moses meets God at a burning bush. It is so
symbolic of Moses's journey to date, and the story
of the rest of his life. He was a man with a burning
sense of justice—hence his action in killing the

Egyptian, which resulted in his journey to Midian. It was a journey undertaken at speed as he literally 'ran for his life'. Here now he meets a most amazing miracle—something which burns but does not consume. He sees, and in the encounter that follows, he is touched by a power which includes that burning sense of justice, yet which is greater than it, namely a heart burning with compassion. A compassion that feels and knows and acts.

Mary's encounter with God is another unique event. It really is uniquely unique, if I may put it like that. To be told that she will become mother of the messiah—without the aid of a human father. No wonder she 'pondered these things in her heart'. It would take her a lifetime to fathom the meaning of this encounter and subsequent experience. The church today, indeed, is still 'pondering these things'.

For us too, the story of our journey in faith is punctuated (given form, structure, and meaning) by our encounters with God. In my first book, *In the Crucible*, I begin that story of a church's encounter with God, by telling my own story of some major encounters with God that have shaped who I am and affected all that I have done. Every believer has their own unique stories to tell.

Prayer as encounter

What has all this consideration of scripture being full of stories, journeys and encounters to do with prayer? Just this: if discipleship is all about story, journey and encounter, then this will also be true of prayer. For prayer gives particular focus to, and expression of, our meeting with God.

Notice at this point, that the encounters which
are recorded in scripture, although they are of limited duration (only Jacob's, of the ones described
above, would have lasted more than a few minutes), they were of lasting impact. As was Isaiah's
vision in the temple which constituted his calling
to the prophetic ministry. Paul's encounter on the
road to Damascus did not last long (falling off
a horse takes 'no time at all'!), but its impact
lasted a lifetime. So with Peter's call to be a fisher
of men.

Encounters with God, in other words, shape
the nature of discipleship. They are foundational
events. They are also model events—they teach
us how God reveals himself, and how he can be
known on a daily basis. Which is why, from both
personal experience, and study of the scriptures, I
have become convinced that we need to see prayer
as encounter with God. It is both one of the fundamental ways in which we meet God, and is also
essential for our reflecting on, and living out our
lives in the light of, such major encounters with
God as we experience. Moreover, it is how we keep
ourselves open to fresh encounters with God—on
the Way.

The structure of encounters

Having established that life is full of encounters
with God we have already gone some way in
answering an objection to seeing encounters as
the key to prayer. That objection is that the
encounters with God I have referred to are such
unique events that there is no consistent pattern

that can be seen in them. Certainly at one level that is so. I doubt whether anyone reading this book has seen a burning bush, been knocked off his horse by the revelation of God, or had an annunciation.

However, what I want to show is that there is a clear structure in all of these encounters and that this structure is a fine framework for personal prayer. I want to draw your attention to a threefold pattern which is evident within any type of encounter with God.

It begins with *seeing*; that is, with an awareness of God himself. Transcendent reality breaks through into the lives of ordinary people. The focus is on God, the Other. This is the nature of worship, which involves our being 'lost in wonder, love and praise' as the hymn puts it. Awareness of God re-orientates us around the fact that God is the centre of the world, and of our world too. The means will vary enormously—burning bushes, temples full of God, angels visiting us, and so forth—but the starting point is the same; there is a seeing of the reality and presence of God. This suggests that personal prayer should begin with worship, with looking away, out and up to God.

Next comes the experience of *knowing* and being known. No one comes out of the experience unchanged. Isaiah is aware of being a man of unclean lips, John on the isle of Patmos 'fell at his feet as though dead', Moses is touched by the justice of God which does not consume but rather burns with compassion. There is often a facing up to, owning and finding transformation from, personal sin. Sometimes it is sin that has lain dormant for decades.

Knowing, in the biblical sense, is that intimacy in which we both know and are known. It expresses the deepest level of taking the truth of God into ourselves, and being changed by it. So, if the first characteristic of these encounters is that of seeing God, the second is that they address us and bring about change in us. This suggests that worship should be followed by openness to God's Word and Spirit to touch, heal, rebuke, strengthen, affirm and direct us.

The final stage is that of *going*. Jacob goes to be reconciled to Esau, Moses goes to Pharaoh to say 'let my people go', Isaiah responds to the call 'who will go for us?' with the declaration 'Lord, here am I send me'. In the New Testament the same pattern holds good. Jesus goes from his baptism to begin his ministry, Peter, after the miraculous catch of fish goes to be a 'fisher of men', Zacchaeus goes to give back to those whom he has robbed.

Service, and costly discipleship, rather than emotional satisfaction and comfort, is the consistent evidence of true encounter with God. Doubtless some of those events were overwhelmingly emotional experiences, but the goal was not the 'feel-good factor' but the 'do-good fact'. True prayer, equally, will issue in a life of obedience. The Anglican liturgy has it right when, after baptism, it speaks of 'fighting under the banner of Christ', and—at the end of the communion service—it sends people out 'in the power of your Spirit to live and work to your praise and glory'. Such going has two parts. There is the initial part, in personal prayer and public worship, of going through intercession—caring for the world around us; and then there is the physical part of going into the world to participate in God's work.

From a different angle

The structure of *seeing*, *knowing* and *going* can be described in three words that are rich words in Christian vocabulary. They are *revelation*, *conversion*, and *mission*. Indeed when we see that this is what encounter with God is about we realise that there are few, if any, places in scripture where at least one of those themes is not evident.

Revelation is the word that scripture uses to describe how we come to see God. In the me-centred culture in which we live prayer is easily reduced to technique. The truth is that our seeing God is first and foremost his gift. The word revelation also reminds us that those moments of seeing are not so much moments when God turns up, as moments when what is already and always present becomes present to us. Elisha's prayer to God for his servant exactly describes our position. It was not a prayer that God might come, but that the servant might have his eyes opened to see the reality of God's presence: 'O Lord, open his eyes so that he may see' (2 Kings 6:17).

In our frustrations in prayer (and even biblical characters had them) we can imagine that God is rather like a camera. He is One whom we can now and again imprint a lasting impression upon, but who is seemingly, for the most part, shut to the cry of our hearts. The truth, I am sure, is actually the opposite. It is we who are so rarely open. The constant light of God's presence finds such limited access to our innermost beings. Like my own camera, we are only open to God for two hundredths of a second once every other month! As T.S. Eliot put it, 'mankind can bear very little reality'. However, it is as we look up that we train ourselves to be in the best place to see God, to experience revelation.

Conversion is a word that describes not just a once in a lifetime's experience, but rather it defines a way of life; a life of continual turning to the light of God's presence. With that turning to the light comes change. Change in who we are, in how we see life, and how we resolve to handle it. Paul puts this process of conversion in these terms; 'And we, who with unveiled faces all reflect the Lord's glory, are being transformed into his likeness with ever-increasing glory, which comes from the Lord, who is the Spirit' (2 Cor 3:18). Truly to pray is to be changed in the process. The human instinct is to come to God so as to bring about change in his attitude to us or action for us. True Christian prayer is the prayer 'Your kingdom come', and 'May it be to me as you have said' (Lk 1:38). As we shall see, the process of turning and being changed is right at the heart of prayer.

Mission is the third word. It points to the fact that there is always a sending out from true encounters with God. It is a sending into his world, his mission, and his will, that we may thereby enter more fully into his presence in the world.

The description in Mark of Jesus' choice of the apostles well expresses this double flow of coming and going which is involved in encounter of God in prayer and life. Mark records: 'He appointed twelve—designating them apostles—that they might be with him and that he might send them out' (Mk 3:14). So, for us, being sent out is one of the marks of authentic prayer to which we will return in due course. More immediately, however, after the prayer exercise which follows, we will explore the first of the elements of encounter, namely our seeing of God.

PRAYER EXERCISE: Milestones

One of the important purposes of prayer is to help us stop, and be aware of life and what is happening to us, in order that we may make a freely chosen response. This exercise is designed to help us get in touch with our journey of faith so far.

It is best done with pen and paper (better still, a journal) at the ready so that you can write down the things that arise which speak to you. First identify the period 'under review'. It might be the time of your first encounter with God, but it may well be best to consider the recent past (the last week, month, year), not least because this is something that we can benefit from doing regularly (once every three to six months).

Having identify the period, then simply review your awareness of what you have experienced and learned over that period, under the three headings of:

Seeing

In what ways have I been aware of God's presence in my life?
– is there any experience which stands out?
– is there something someone said or wrote which has struck a chord in me?
– is there a scripture or insight that is memorable?
Make a note of anything, and give thanks for all that is good in your experience.

Knowing

In what ways have I experienced change within
myself?
— in my attitude to God, myself, or others?
— what are the positive/growth changes?
— are there any signs of negative or stuck responses
   in me?
Thank God for his presence in your life, in the joys
and the struggles.

Going

In what ways have I been stepping out in faith
during this period?
Can I identify any sense of *going*?
— give thanks to God for that, and reaffirm your
   commitment to continue.
Are there ways in which I have sensed God's call
to go, but not yet gone?
— bring that before God, affirming your confidence
   in his ability to help.
Are there ways that you sense God sending you
out in the light of this time?
— to say something to someone, or to take some
   deliberate action
— note it and be specific about when, where and
   how action can be taken.

Note: this is not to be an inquisition in which
you criticise yourself for how you have failed,
but rather a trusting review before the One who
is *for* you. Listening more fully to the One who
is Love.

PART TWO

SEEING

Chapter 3

Ways into Seeing

He counted addiction to prayer
not so much the aid of his episcopate
as the delight of his soul
(said of a cardinal in the Vatican at the time of
the Reformation)

Worship is a form of orienteering, for we travel
through life rather like a blind person finding their way along a street. Such a person will be
rehearsing to themselves how many paces before
the kerb, where the next lamppost is, and where
they next need to turn right. Worship has such
a role in the life of the believer. It reminds us
where we are. Worship puts us in touch with
the things which help and guide, alerts us to
what is harmful, and points us to the Centre of
the universe—and of our lives. It is orienteering
in a universe where physical sight is dangerous,
because we easily conclude that 'what you see is
what you get'. In fact, as Elisha's servant found
out, there is a holy art to true seeing (2 Kings
6), which is itself a gift of God. We can confi-
dently ask for the gift of such seeing. As Paul
puts it:

So we fix our eyes not on what is seen, but on
   what is unseen.
For what is seen is temporary, but what is
   unseen is eternal.

(2 Cor 4:18)

What we have established so far is that the first
stage in a true meeting with God begins with God
himself, and with our *seeing* him. For to see God is
to recognise him for who he is, the Sovereign Lord,
'high and lifted up' (Is 6:1) as Isaiah expresses
it. Seeing God as the centre of the universe, and
therefore as the centre of my world of relationships
and responsibilities, is to be converted: turned
around to see the One from whom all life comes.
It is also liberation from self-centredness. Which
is why, in every age, the first requirement for the
creature is to acknowledge the Creator. This is so,
not because *he* needs our worship, but because
we do.

   How does this work out in the prayer life of
the Christian today? Here we turn to the practice
of worship, or *seeing* as I have called it, in the
pattern of our prayer encounter with God. In the
next chapter we will explore one particular way
in which we can 'enter his courts with praise'. It
is based on Revelation chapters four and five and
is called 'Beholding the Throne'. Here, however, I
want to explore other ways in which we can train
ourselves to focus first on God, before proceeding
further in prayer. They are as follows:

The celebration of stillness

We live in a frantic world, where we are in
danger of losing touch with the sheer gift of

life. We risk the possibility of becoming 'human doings' rather than 'human beings'. So we need to re-learn what it is to live in the moment, to receive life as a gift to be enjoyed rather than a problem to be solved, and to enjoy who we are and what we have received. In other words we need to learn how to celebrate sabbath. For not only did God rest on the seventh day, but throughout creation we are told that 'he saw that it was good' (Gen 1:10, 12, 18, 21, 25, concluding with v 31 'God saw all that he had made, and it was very good'. He took time to meditate on all his works; to enjoy the process as much as the product.

One way for us to 'step out of ourselves' is to still our hearts, look up to God, and slowly and quietly give thanks for all that is. Yes, it is all right to begin with ourselves. Thank God for our breathing, for such health and mental faculties as we have. But we go beyond that, making connection with all that is. This is what the Old Testament concept of shalom—peace—is all about. This can include the warmth and furnishing of the room, our 'loved ones', and human society. We can thank God for the gift of the government. That might seem like a difficult task, but a moment's reflection on the recent history of Lebanon and the former state of Yugoslavia, reminds us all too vividly of the hell of no government.

Beyond that, we can step out and 'make connection' with creation: whether as expressed in pictures on our walls, or pictures in our prayer journal (yes, put in the 'views' which speak to you), or simply in our imagination. It may not just be a view as such (e.g. Mount Everest), but rather a location that we associate with an experience

of connectedness with all that is—a moment of
shalom.

Little, if any, of this needs to be with spoken
words. We can practise looking, remembering,
and imagining, with praise and gratitude to the
Creator and Giver of the gifts we are enjoying.

In this way we are stilling our hearts, stopping
the rush of modern society that disorientates us,
and coming in touch with the child within. And
we need a little child to lead us, for it is the child
who knows how to play, how to enjoy the present
moment, and how to be in touch with the wonder of
it all. If we do use words, it could be by repeating,
from the liturgy: 'Lift up your hearts, we lift them
to the Lord' as the only words we use while making
this journey of adoration to the Author of life. In so
doing we discover him restoring in us the capacity
to wonder, to enjoy, and to be still. Above all, this
journey out from self to the Centre, needs to take
us through connection with all created reality, into
the presence of the Creator and Giver of All.

Devotional Psalms

Another, and more familiar, way of entering into
God's presence is to make use of the devotional
psalms. The more I have studied the psalms and
discussed their use with people the more I have
become convinced that the list of such psalms is
not as fixed as one might think. Some people
find one psalm 'devotional' and others not. By
'devotional' I mean, a psalm that takes us into
God—turns our attention to him and assists our
seeing him. We will see, in Chapter Seven (Praying Back the Scriptures), more about how best to

pray the scriptures—rather than just read them.
However, for those not familiar with such a list
here are the first dozen I use. Psalms 8, 16, 19,
23, 24, 25, 27, 29, 33, 23, 34, 40, 42. It would be
best for you however to develop your own list.

The psalms have always played a large part
in the spiritual disciplines and prayer life of the
church. It is clear from Jesus' prayer life that the
psalms were both his Prayer Book and his Hymn
Book. The monastic movement has made the use
of the psalms a major feature of its daily worship.
Indeed some parts of the Orthodox Church used
to require of anyone seeking ordination, that they
be able to recite all 150 psalms! Certainly we can
benefit greatly if we learn some psalms by heart,
and pray them with our heart. It is then quite
possible to use the psalm whilst driving, or having
a bath, or whatever, because we have it written
on our heart. I use Psalm 45 like this. Not that I
claim to know it word for word, but—as we shall
see below—I know the structure and the content
sufficiently that is spurs on worship in my own
words.

The liturgy of the heart

Here I want to pause in the flow of considering
various ways into seeing, in order to spell out a second prayer principle that can aid us greatly in this
work. It may sound strange to some people's ears
that liturgy and healing have any connection—
especially in the context of personal prayer. But
they do, or rather they can. In the following way.

There is an ancient 'liturgical principle' on which,
for example, the Anglican Church has built not

just its worship but its doctrine too. The principle,
in its Latin form, is *lex orandi, lex credendi*, which
means '*the word spoken is the word believed*'.
The principle is that what we say regularly and
build into our unconscious and subconscious has
a powerful and formative effect on us. It shapes
our thinking, behaviour and belief. It is for this
reason that the Anglican Church does not have
a 'doctrinal basis', for it sees that its doctrine is
enshrined in its liturgy.

PRAYER PRINCIPLE TWO
WRITE THE TRUTH IN OUR HEARTS
*Learning prayers by heart plants truths as
seeds within that can help us to enjoy their
fruit at any time.*

However, many people today—particularly those
influenced by charismatic renewal—falsely imagine that the only form of prayer is spontaneous
prayer. That is an important element of prayer,
but so is the prayer of the heart that arises out
of what we have consciously sown in it. If we will
but write things that really matter in our hearts,
we will find them becoming a well of living water;
especially when we are in desert places.

Sight: using an icon

Here is one of those 'spiritual exercises' I referred
to in the introduction. Sadly, for many of us in
the West, and especially those nurtured in the
evangelical and renewal traditions of the church,
we have become deeply captive to the culture
in ways we often miss. In particular, we have

become trapped within a narrowly rational way of understanding reality, and into a consequent restriction of communication to words alone. Yes, the word of God is foundational to the gospel, and to Christian living. Yes, God and creation can be understood—to some degree—by rational thought. But we have lost sight of the greater truth of the Word-made-flesh. Jesus, after all, is the living icon (image/likeness) of the Father.

PRAYER OF THE HEART:
Seeing God.

Holy God, holy and mighty,
holy and immortal,
Have mercy on us.

(The 'trisagion' ['thrice-holy'] chant of the Orthodox church which has been sung for well over one thousand years.)

For us there is a tendency to take icons too literally. We only see them as *pictures*. We need to know that that is not how the Orthodox Church handles them. In that tradition people are told: 'When you pray, stand before an icon, *close your eyes*, and pray to the Father in heaven.' That should alert us to the fact that something other than the worship of the icon is going on.

The reason for the instruction of closing your eyes is because an icon is not seen as a picture on the wall, but a *window* into heaven. We are to 'see through' (as we say) the icon: seeing through to the truth portrayed in it. Jesus was doing this all the time in his parables. He was seeing through the fragile existence of the sparrow to the faithfulness of the One who cares for it, he was seeing through

the work of the sower, to the greater work of the
Sower of all creation and creativity.

Indeed, even 'window' is not sufficient to describe the role of an icon, for they are intended to
be a *door* that leads us into the presence of God.
They fulfil the role of the open door in heaven
through which John 'saw' the glory of heaven's
praises—as we shall see in the next chapter. So
too, an icon can lead us into the presence of God.

The Oaks of Mamre

Consider, for example, the best known icon in the
West at present, namely Rublev's icon called 'The
Oaks of Mamre' (it is reproduced on the back cover
so that you can use it to aid your seeing of God).
It represents the story of the three visitors whom
Abraham and Sarah had when they 'entertained
angels unawares' (Gen 18). Those visitors came to
tell them that they would have a son within the
year—at which news Sarah laughed.

Orthodox spirituality sees in those visitors a
picture of the Trinity. Rublev represents them sitting before a table with a chalice on it (remember
Abraham went and killed an animal for the meal).
On the right-hand side is a figure clothed in green
and blue robes. Those robes represent the green of
earth and the blue of heaven. It is the figure of the
Holy Spirit. He is both the One who comes from
heaven (blue), as the communicator of divinity
to humanity, and yet also the One at home on
earth (green), for he was the agent of creation
when the world was made, and when the Son
was conceived (Gen 1:2, and Lk 1:35). He is the
One who introduces us to the Godhead.

In this icon, the figure representing the Holy

Spirit has his head bowed towards the person in the centre, robed partly in blue and partly in the royal robes of empire. This is the figure of Jesus. The One who, in a unique way came from heaven, but who now has returned to glory as the all-conquering king who overcame through death, defeating evil by the power of unselfish, sacrificial and forgiving love. His head is also bowed, as he looks to the figure on the left of the picture.

This third figure is robed in translucent robes that speak of an inner glory which shines for ever. Here the Father is seated in majesty, yet also as the One who visits this earth. Remember 'God was reconciling the world to himself in Christ' (2 Cor 5:19, my italics).

These figures are seated in a circle, but it is not a completed or closed circle. It is a 'C' not an 'O'. The whole picture invites us in—to complete the circle, to be part of the life of mutual love, affirmation, and creativity which characterised the interaction within the Trinity. What an immense and incredible privilege. This is the source of vitality for all living. No wonder we can simply stand before such a presence and, without a word, enter in through the door of adoration.

Delight

A further way into the presence of God which enables us to 'take delight in the Lord' (Ps 37:4; a phrase worth studying throughout the psalm as an aid to worship itself), is by means of the image of marriage as it applies to the church's relationship with God. It is a picture used widely in scripture.

Psalm 45 is a wedding psalm that is also what

I call an 'encounter psalm' for it expresses the
three phases of encounter. The first part of the
psalm (45:1–9) sings the praises of the king who
is about to be married: this is the *seeing* phase.
The next part of the psalm (45:10–15) is addressed
to the bride, who through marriage is about to
have her whole identity changed and bound up
with that of the king: this is the *knowing and
being known* phase of encounter with God. The
last part (45:16–17) speaks of the fruit of this
union, the children who will be born to the royal
couple: this is the *going* phase of encounter. It
is a wonderful psalm for re-orientating ourselves
around the reality of God and his love for us.

The Song of Songs is a whole book devoted to the
love relationship of marriage. It found a place in
scripture partly because the Jewish people were at
home in creation and the natural world—they did
not suffer from the dualism evident in the Greek
culture which has so influenced our present way
of seeing life. That Greek notion made such a
distinction between the physical and spiritual,
that it created a conflict between them. To the
Hebrew mind reality can be seen as having layers
of meaning bound up in the one event; the physical
in the spiritual and the spiritual in the physical.
The Hebrew mind was well able to see God and
his goodness and generosity mirrored in human
loving. However, there was another reason for the
book's inclusion in the Old Testament scriptures.
It was included primarily because it was seen as
describing the relationship between Israel and
her God.

The marriage theme is continued throughout
the New Testament. Jesus speaks of himself as
the Bridegroom whom they will not always have

with them (Mk 2:19). Paul, in writing about the
marriage relationship, points beyond it in his
great passage in Ephesians, when he concludes
with the words: 'This is a profound mystery—but
I am talking about Christ and the church' (Eph
5:32). He also uses the marriage relationship in a
striking way in Romans (7:1–4). Finally, scripture
ends with the vision of the marriage supper of the
Lamb, and 'the new Jerusalem, coming down out
of heaven from God, prepared as a bride beauti-
fully dressed for her husband' (Rev 21:2).

On several occasions in my prayer pilgrimage
I have used Watchman Nee's little commentary
The Song of Songs (Christian Literature Crusade,
London. '65) to take me through that book, a little
at a time. It took about three months the last time
I did it. But why rush a good meal? To take
delight in the Lord is to enjoy both him and
his love for us. Prayer is an experience, quite
intense at times—though often, in my experience,
not for long—in which we encounter Love in its
richest form.

We need to slow down, however, if we are to
touch such moments; but they are part of God's
good plan for us. Sadly we are often in so much
of a hurry that we rush into God's presence,
deliver our message (about our need, or our pre-
ferred solution to some issue) and depart, without
ever having said 'hello' or enjoyed the One who
loves us.

Silence

There is a certain progression in the stages of seeing God which are built into the logic of the steps

we have been through, from celebration through
psalms, and sight, to delight and silence. The
important point is to be aware of these elements,
for then we shall be able to recognise the voice of
the One who loves us when we realise he is calling
us on into delight or silence.

I have little to say about silence, after all words
seem hardly appropriate, but I have recently seen
that it is not so much a straight line, from celebration to silence, as a circle. For silence encapsulates
the capacity to be still and to enjoy the present
moment—as the Moment of the Presence. So we
need to do some 'stillness' exercises.

I have found some of the following helpful. For,
for a number of months I carried around this
quotation from Dr Clyde Filby, which helped me to
still the inner turmoil and the instinctive rushing
on to the 'next business':

> Once every day I shall simply stare at a tree,
> a flower, a cloud, or a person. I shall not then
> be concerned to at all to ask *what* they are but
> simply be glad *that* they are.
>
> (Quoted by Leanne Payne in *The Healing
> Presence* [Kingsway Publications,
> Eastbourne. '89] p. 161)

Another exercise is to read the poem that follows,
simply as a way of slowing down. It says, at one
level, nothing about God or worship, or adoration.
Yet God reveals himself in the whole of his creation—as does any artist—and we do indeed meet
him there. Yet I do not read the poem *in order
to meet God*—that turns it into technique and
discipline. I read it rather to slow myself down,
to enter into delight, into the present moment, and

into awareness of the wonder of creation. For that
is a place where God so often is discovered. So such
an exercise in stillness leads me into celebration
and so back into the other ways of seeing. May
that be your experience too. Track the steps and
paths that God takes you on as you take delight
in the Lord and learn to 'be still and know that
I am God' (Ps 46:10):

> What is this life if full of care,
> We have no time to stand and stare?
>
> No time to stand beneath the boughs
> and stare as long as sheep and cows.
>
> No time to see, when woods we pass,
> where squirrels hide their nuts in grass:
>
> No time to see in broad daylight,
> streams full of stars, like skies at night:
>
> No time to turn at Beauty's glance,
> And watch her feet, how they can dance:
>
> No time to wait till her mouth can
> Enrich that smile her eyes began?
>
> A poor life this, if full of care,
> We have no time to stand and stare.
>
> (*Leisure*, by William Henry Davies)

PRAYER EXERCISE: Calling on the name of the Lord

This is a way of developing what I call a liturgy of
the heart; that is words and forms of prayer that
are so written on our hearts that they spring up
like wells of living water from within us.

Another name for this exercise is *the grammar
of praise*, for it focuses on:
nouns, the names we give God,
adjectives, which describe the way we see God's
character, and
verbs, which tell how we see God at work.
The exercise concludes with our *response* of adoration, in words, or silent enjoyment and seeing
of God.

Sit down, relax your body, let go of distracting
thoughts and tasks, and receive and welcome
God's presence—by faith, whatever the feelings
are.

His name is wonderful

Then *call on the name of the Lord* by repeating the
following titles of God: **Rock, Light, Shepherd,
Friend, Creator**.
  Repeat them slowly, savouring them, picturing
the title used and then moving to the next one.
Once you have these five names you can develop
two further exercises.
a. *add your response*: such as after 'Shepherd' you
      may want to say 'thank you that you know me
      by name' and 'thank you that you care'. Keep
      your response short, do not strive in any way.
      If words dry up, move back into the rhythm of
      the names.
b. *add your own list of names* (or substitute them
      for the ones I have suggested).

The Holy One

Next (at the same 'sitting', or at another time, maybe after a month of doing the first part), do the same exercise, this time focusing on God's character. Here is the list to get you started: **Holy, joyful, faithful, creative, mighty**.
Again, take the words slowly,
– taking them into yourself, memorising them, and chewing them over.
– add your own further adjectives and responses as before.

The God who acts

The final part is as above, but using verbs to describe what God does. Here is the list to get you started: **The One who sets free, shakes, calls, speaks, loves**
– words that tell us who he is, what his character is, and how he reveals himself to us.

Chapter 4

Beholding the Throne

The way to overcome gravity—and so much triviality—is to arise in the Presence each morning.
David Adam, *The Cry of the Deer* (Triangle/ SPCK, London: '87) p. 15

Forfeit your sense of awe, let your conceit diminish your ability to revere, and the universe becomes a marketplace for you.
Rabbi Heschel: *The Earth is the Lord's* (Farrar, Straus & Giroux, New York: '78)

Whilst worship is essential to life, holiness and health in every age, there are two particular reasons why this is especially true today.

Over the course of the last few hundred years there has been a strange twist in the development of human consciousness and the human perception of reality—at least in Western culture. It is this. When people thought that the earth was the centre of the universe, with the sun, moon and stars all orbiting around planet earth, they had no difficulty in grasping the fact that God is the true centre of all created order, and that—for sheer survival—we are to give God his rightful worship, and the obedience of our lives to his revealed will.

Yet, since scientists discovered that the earth is just one of several planets circling one not particularly special star, somewhat to the edge of a galaxy which is part of a family of millions of galaxies, we have—at a deep psychological level—functioned as though *we* are the centre of the world. Or rather, because of our individualism, we instinctively act as though *I* am the centre of reality. This self-centred view of reality is one of the primary characteristics of our culture.

It is therefore vital that we break out of that false notion that we are converted from the surrounding culture's view of reality, to the truth that God is the centre of all that is. In an address in 1993 to the Congress of European Bishops, Cardinal Basil Hume said:

> In a world that is seen by many to have no ultimate purpose or value, the Self is seen as providing the only realm in which our experience can have meaning. No authority external to the individual is acknowledged.

Indeed, the Christian community needs to be aware of how far this 'self-centred' view of reality has permeated our thinking. Tom Smail, in his book *The Forgotten Father*, expresses well how this worldview has affected the Renewal movement:

> The crucial question that the whole renewal faces is whether renewed people will be led only as far as their own felt needs take them, or whether they will go on in obedience to the

Father who wants to make them a sign to the
world of his transforming and revolutionary
power in Christ.
(Tom Smail, *The Forgotten Father* [Hodder &
                     Stoughton, London. '80] p. 180)

Spiritual orientation

The other particular reason why worship is needed
as a healing gift in our culture is that the
trends towards secularisation and materialism
have eaten away at the sense of awe, wonder and
transcendence that are all around us in the universe, and for which the human spirit hungers.

An African bishop said recently 'You West-
erners are so busy counting your pennies, you
have lost the art of counting your blessings!' We
have lost touch with the spiritual dimension of
all reality. But things are changing—though not
necessarily for the better. There is now a growing
spiritual awareness, hunger and interest in our
society. However, because it is happening in the
context of a self-focused, self-aware, and self-
centred culture, there is an inevitable tendency
to look for that spiritual dimension within. This
is the basis of New Age spirituality.

Typical of this approach was the comment of the
leader of a New Age community, who said on TV
recently that, as she listened to the voices within
her, she realised not just that this was God, but
that, as she put it, 'as Jesus said, "the Father
and I are one", so I now realise that I am my
own divinity, I do not need to look outside for the
Divine'. That horrific misreading of scripture, and
of one's own nature, is best addressed by a strong

focus on the Otherness and transcendent glory of God. This is where prayer must begin.

Yes, God does dwell with us, and in us: yet he is also, and essentially, beyond us and other than us. In technical terms his imminence is a consequence of his prior transcendence. In other words, God exists before, beyond, and apart from his creation, before he becomes present to it and to humans in it. His presence flows out of his otherness. Once we let go of the fact that he is our Father *in heaven*, we become disconnected from him and turn our search towards 'the divine within'. Indeed I see that this could become the Achilles heel of the charismatic movement with its love of an informality which domesticates God.

We are in urgent need of seeing God in his transcendent glory. Which is why the discipline of looking away from self and seeing God is vital to prayer, and to our sheer survival as worshipping creatures.

One particular way

The practice of beholding the throne is based on Revelation chapters four and five which reveal the worship of God in eternity. It takes us into the realm of the unseen which is true and unchanging reality. The focus of that world is the glory of the Father, the wonder of the Lamb slain from the foundation of the world, and the sevenfold active presence of the Holy Spirit.

In taking this outer-directed step of focus upon God, it is important to remember that Jesus not only taught us to begin our prayers by saying 'Our Father in heaven', but also began his own prayers

in the same way. For example at the conclusion
of the mission of the disciples, Jesus prays: 'I
praise you, Father, Lord of heaven and earth . . .'
(Matt 11:25). In his prayer as recorded in John
chapter 17, we are told: 'After Jesus said this, he
looked towards heaven and prayed: "Father . . ."'
(Jn 17:1). Revelation chapters four and five simply give us a permanent record of the heavenly
vision that was, for a moment, opened up to
Isaiah (Is 6). It is now written down for our
learning.

As we behold the throne we are doing what the
apostle Paul told us to do, namely to:

'set your hearts on things above, where Christ
is seated at the right hand of God' (Col 3:1)

The writer of the epistle to the Hebrews encour-
ages us in similar words when he writes:

'Fix your thoughts on Jesus, the apostle and
high priest whom we confess' (Heb 3:1)
'Let us fix our eyes on Jesus, the author and
perfecter of our faith' (Heb 12:2)

To do so is to be liberated from self-concern and
self-centredness, and to enter more fully into
likeness to Christ. This is the law of unconscious
assimilation. We become like those whom we
spend most meaningful and frequent time with.

Like exiles, we long for our homeland ('our
citizenship is in heaven', Phil 3:20). As we behold the throne we live in the 'presence of the
future'. We are preparing, as the exiles of eternity

(1 Pet 1:1–2), for the everlasting worship of God
in heaven.

Brief overview

It is helpful to have some understanding of the
place of these two chapters in the Book of Revelation, and of the way in which they balance each
other.

John, suffering persecution and imprisonment
for the faith along with many others, is on the isle
of Patmos. There he has a vision of Christ in glory.
This encounter with the risen Lord causes him to
fall down as if dead. However, he is raised up to
be told that he is about to see 'what is to come';
with a view to his sharing that with the embat-
tled churches of the region. He then receives an
individual letter for each of those seven churches.
Letters which are incisive, affirming, and specific
to each location.

After this personal encounter, and these words
to the local churches, the scene moves to the glory
of heaven. That is the focus of chapters four and
five, to which we will return shortly. After those
chapters comes a series of bewildering (to the
modern reader) and graphic visions of the spiritual
conflict of the End Times, culminating in the fall
of Babylon (Rome, symbol of the principalities and
powers), the marriage supper of the Lamb, the
coming of the New Jerusalem and the invitation
of the Spirit and Bride to 'Come' into the kingdom
prepared for those who are called.

Chapters four and five are therefore the hinge
chapters. Chapter four begins with an open door,
through which John steps and sees the glory of
all that is. He sees the creative, yet unchanging,

reality of heaven. The key to chapter four is that everything is seen in relation to the throne. In meditating upon it, it has the power to integrate our living and give us connectedness with all that is.

The mood changes in chapter five. There is a great sense of *being* in chapter four. Chapter five is about *doing*, about the work of creation, namely the re-creation of everything through the death and resurrection of Christ (the Lamb). The key is the opening of the scroll, which is the symbol of the unfolding of God's purposes in his world. The grief which John experiences is because it seems that no one can open those scrolls (that is, fulfil God's plan for his world). Grief turns to joy with the arrival of the Lion of the tribe Judah.

Chapter four then, before the Throne, celebrates the being of God as Centre of all that is. Chapter five, the unfolding of his redeeming work in history. This balance of being and doing defines the nature of the whole cosmos—stillness of being, and purposefulness in creativity—and our natures too. As we meditate on these scriptures we are put in touch with these sources of healing life by relationship to the One from whom they come.

Entering in with the imagination

What follows is designed to help us enter, in imagination and spirit, into the centre of reality and in the process to be re-orientated around unseen reality, through meditation on Revelation chapters four and five.

Here we need some muscle-stretching prayer-exercise. The muscles I refer to are our imaginations. For the fact is that modern life leaves

little or nothing to the imagination; it does it all
for us. This is partly because our culture has
been (it is changing) very rational. So, typically
today, when we read, we read 'literally'. We are
at home with the handbook for the video or the
freezer. It tells us the mechanics of how the
thing works. It requires no imagination to read.
Likewise our entertainment leaves little to the
imagination—not least in the 'literal portrayal'
of sex and violence. As a society, our imagination
has been starved, and our ability to imagine has
atrophied. Which is where the Holy Spirit comes
to our aid in prayer. It is he who enables us to
feel, and sense, and imagine a situation. We can
ask him for help when we find our imagination
weak.

Practical matters

Here again, the principle of 'counting the steps'
being the stage before dancing, is an important
one to bear in mind. In other words, do not be
surprised if you find this exercise 'awkward',
'self-conscious', 'artificial' or 'not me'. That is
an inevitable part of the learning phase.

The first stage is to use the words given, and
then—as you make it your own—use a prayer
journal to record your own thoughts and ways
of meditating. You may find it helpful to write
out simply the text of scripture given below on a
page or two of your journal, and then add your
own commentary or 'aid to meditation' yourself.
What follows is intended to get your imagination
started. As we have already seen, it is important
to write the text of scripture on our heart. I am

now able to sit on a bus or train, and enter into
this meditation, simply because I have done it
sufficiently often to have the scriptures on 'instant
recall'.

You may also find it helpful to take one section
at a time and mediate on it over several prayer
times before moving on to the next. When I began
doing it I did the first section for a few weeks,
and then added the second, and then the third.
To make it manageable I then dropped the first
and added the fourth. Eventually I got to the last
section, by which time I was still doing only three
at a time. As you work on this material over a
sustained period (a number of weeks) you will
find it becoming increasingly your own. You will
then need the notes less and less, and find your
own way more and more.

John Talbot (founder of the Brothers and Sisters
of Charity), has the following wise and encouraging words to say about this repeated engaging
with, and memory of, scripture:

> One of the ways to control the mind is by
> good Christian meditation. This means tak-
> ing the time intentionally to fill our minds
> and thoughts with the ways of Jesus Christ.
> This is done by meditating on the Scriptures.
> . . . When we do this as an intentional disci-
> pline, we discover that our thoughts will soon
> begin going to Jesus on their own in their
> wanderings. Once we train the mind to take
> this journey through intentional discipline,
> it will begin doing it on its own by way of
> habit.
>
> (John Talbot, *Blessings*
> [St. Paul Publications, UK '91] p. 97)

However, do remember that internalising these things does take time. How often did you repeat your two times tables before they became part of you? Beholding the throne is a more difficult, and more vital, task, but it happens in the same way.

Repeat each verse of scripture several times, read the meditation slowly seeking to 'see' and enter into this vision, repeating the scripture as frequently as you feel comfortable with. End by saying the scripture 'by heart'. Do not be concerned to meditate and memorise; become comfortable with the memorising first, and then the mediation on the scripture will grow.

PRAYER PRINCIPLE THREE
SOWING AND REAPING TAKE TIME
In our mechanical world we expect the light to come up as soon as we flick the switch
Prayer functions in the realm of relationships and growing things
You reap what you sow—but not the same day!
Growing things take time to develop.
Sowing requires faith

PRAYER EXERCISE: Beholding the throne

There before me was an open door . . .
'Come up here and I will show you what must take place after this' (Rev 4:1)

See the open door as large and looking out onto a vast (outdoor) scene

– we are not entering in, so much as coming out
   in the open, to enjoy God and all that is.
Hear the open invitation: the angel's summons to
   Come.
– it is personal, caring, yet with great (divine)
   authority.
– sense the honour of the invitation; you have
   personally been called before God.
Be aware that this is a journey in time; to gain a
   foretaste of where the world is going.
– know that you have this foretaste of the desti-
   nation to help you recognise the Way there.
This is a glimpse of glory, of what is lasting in life,
   and of where you are heading.

At once I was in the Spirit (Rev 4:2a)

Relax; prayer is the gift of God.
See yourself as in a sailing boat carried by the
   wind of the Spirit into the Father's presence.
– 'I am a feather in the breathe of God', said St
   Hildegrade of Bingen.
– see yourself carried by the Spirit, into the glory
   of what is to come.
Remember the icon of the Trinity and that the
   Spirit is drawing you into the unending flow of
   love, and unity, and creativity in the Godhead.

There before me was a throne in heaven
with someone sitting on it (Rev 4:2b)

Rejoice, all that is, is no accident; there is a Hand
   on the helm of the universe.
– there is a throne, and One who is in control.
– it is none other than the 'God and Father of our
   Lord Jesus Christ'. Everything in this passage

is related to the throne ('surrounding', 'from',
'before', etc).
– let the tide of this reality flood out into your life
and world.
– everything that is, finds its identity in relation
to God.
Sense the awe and wonder of this divine Centre
of all that is.
– feel the vastness of the universe finding its
point of origin, direction, and meaning from the
Person who is seated on the throne.

**One who sat there had the appearance of
jasper and camelian.
A rainbow, resembling an emerald, en-
circled the throne.** (Rev 4:3)

Colour is now added to our vision of God in glory.
– see the rich colours building to the centre of the
universe.
Let the richness of colour shake you free of any
dull vision of God.
– he is the source of life and light and glory and
joy and wonder.

Creation reflects something of the brilliance of his
being.
– do not try to 'work out' how a rainbow can be
green (emerald), but rejoice in the brilliance and
beauty of all creation.
See the beauty of any part of creation which
has touched you, coming before God to worship
him.

**Surrounding the throne were twenty-four
. . . elders.**

They were dressed in white and had crowns of gold on their heads. (Rev 4:4)

How wonderful that humanity is included, not excluded, by God's presence.
– what cost he bore to count us in on his eternal purposes.
The elders are the patriarchs of the Old Covenant, and the apostles of the New.
– they are our patriarchs and apostles: we rejoice for them, and in them.
– imagine the look in their eyes, their love for God, their rejoicing in the end of the story of which they were such a vital part.
Know that God counts all believers in on that same story.
– he clothes us with righteousness so that we can enter.
– the robes he has put on are not outward show, but robes that penetrate the heart.

From the throne came flashes of lightning, rumblings and peals of thunder. (Rev 4:5)

Creation is gathered up into God's presence.
– together with the vastness of space
– the depths of the ocean
– the molten fire a thousand miles thick which begins twenty miles below our feet
– and the delicacy of desert flower and the beauty of the sea horse.
The trees of the field and the rivers clap their hands
– the roaring lion gives praise to God; as do the planets singing on their way.

– even the stones cry out to the source of all being.
Know that this overwhelming power is always and
only used in love.
– in fallen humanity we are trapped and dimin-
   ished by the love of power.
– in divine glory we are touched and made whole
   by the power of love.
See this holy and loving power as able to gather
up the most broken parts of creation
– and bring it to wholeness in Christ.
All creation is gathered up in the vision of God on
the throne.
– in Christ, we are all part of this amazing End
   Time scene.
Now we see it with our imagination; one day we
will literally enter in.

**Before the throne, seven lamps were blaz-
ing. These are the seven spirits of God.**
(Rev 4:5)

See the Spirit as so all-enveloping and active
that he can only be described by the perfect
number (7).
He is fire: the fire that does not consume.
– the fire of the burning bush, and of the burning
   fiery furnace that did not consume, the fire
   within Jesus on the Mount of Transfiguration,
   and the fire that fell at Pentecost.
He is light, shining love and truth into our lives,
and wisdom on the path before us.
– there is no darkness of human distress, evil,
   destructiveness and injustice he cannot penetrate with light: see that light entering the
   dark places you are aware of in the world.

In the centre, around the throne, were four living creatures, and they were covered with eyes. (Rev 4:6)

As the cherubim on the Ark of the covenant witnessed to the presence of the Creator of all so now these creatures witness to God's redeeming purposes for all creation
– 'to bring all things in heaven and on earth together under one head, even Christ'.
(Eph 1:10)
Rejoice in this good news for a suffering world
– 'the whole creation has been groaning as in the pains of childbirth'. (Rom 8:22)
Let the hope of Christ's return lighten your heart with the good that is to come
– 'the creation waits in eager expectation for the sons of God to be revealed' (Rom 8:19)

'Do not weep! See, the Lion of the tribe of Judah, the Root of David, has triumphed. (Rev 5:5)

Feel the distress of John that 'no one was found who was worthy to open the scroll'.
Then rejoice with him as he hears afresh this proclamation of the gospel.
Marvel that the Lion and the Lamb lay down together in the person of Christ (Rev 5:5–6).
Enter into the continual celebration in heaven that the victory has been won.
– we are on the winning side; and the best is yet to be.
By our baptism we have participated in Christ's victory;

– and have been taken up into heaven to rejoice
  and be with him.

**The four living creatures said, 'Amen,'
and the elders fell down and worshipped.**
(Rev 5:14)

Lift up your heart in praise to God for who he is
and what he has done.
– join in the celebration of all creation
– remember that 'Amen' is a triumphant 'yes' to
  all God's purposes, nature and work.

Scattered in the text of these two chapters are *the
five songs of Revelation 4 and 5*
– they are affirmation of God's glory.
– the first two speak of God as the Creator of all.
  (Rev 4:8, and 4:11)
– the second two speak of Jesus as Redeemer. (Rev
  5:9–10, and Rev 5:12)
– the last one speaks of Father and Son in all their
  glory as Creator and Redeemer. (Rev 5:13)
Each of these songs is rightly the basis for meditative entering into the glory of God in their own
right and can form the basis of a complete exercise
of *seeing* God. Take time to savour them and be at
home in their truths which pull us out of ourselves
into holy self-forgetfulness.

PART THREE

KNOWING

Chapter 5

Called By Love
Finding Ourselves Through Encounter with God

*There can be no love of others,
much less love of God
unless there is a self to do the loving.*
Roberti Bondi, *To Pray and to love* p.77

*We can desire to become the Beloved only
when we know that we already are
the Beloved*
Henri Nouwen, *Life of the Beloved*
(Hodder & Stoughton, London. '92) p. 43

Prayer is an affair of the heart, the primary means of both discovering our identity, and yet not being bound by it. Personal health and growth involves both aspects of the paradox of being sure of who I am, and becoming different. That paradox was well expressed in a prayer meeting I attended a number of years ago. Someone prayed 'Lord we thank you for accepting us just as we are'. It was a valid and important truth to express to God in prayer. However, it was followed immediately with the heartfelt response of another person who prayed: 'And thank you, Lord, for not leaving us where we are.'

Self-acceptance and openness to change are both vital ingredients of prayer. We will explore both in this chapter, for prayer, like any intimate relationship, has built into it the dynamic of the heart's hunger, expressed in the cry 'Tell me who I am'.

Discovering identity in prayer

Modern people are profoundly shaped by a man whose name they may never have heard of—Descartes. René Descartes was a seventeenth-century philosopher who propounded the dictum, 'I think, therefore I am'. It has had an amazing impact on how we in the Western world see and understand ourselves. In propounding that dictum, Descartes was saying that we find our identity within. We are the starting point of our own identity.

Scripture, and modern psychology, disagree. Both argue that we are beings-in-relationship, who discover our identity through relationship. The foundational relationship is with what is known as our 'primary care-givers'—normally our parents. It is they who, in a multitude of ways, both give us permission to be ourselves, and help us to discover who we are. They call us into being.

Or they fail to do that. Families where such healthy identity is not discovered, are called 'dysfunctional families', they simply do not do the basic job they are designed for. They can have a crippling effect on a person's being and well-being. Which is where the good news of God's love comes in. His love calls us into being. It is without variation, it is not meeting its own needs, and it gives us permission and encouragement to discover and be who we are.

If we have travelled any distance in *seeing God*, as explored in Part Two, then it will have been having its effect on our self-understanding. Because we are beings-in-relationship we tend to be a 'different person' with each person to whom we relate. This can be destructive, if we are trying to please everyone we meet (or trying to control everyone we meet), because we end up having 'no fixed abode' within.

It can also be a sign of health and a gift to our health. If everyone we meet draws out of us some aspect of our nature, then life will enrich us at every turn—yes, even if what another person draws out of us is our anger and frustration! What makes the differences? It is that there is a secure 'self to do the loving' as Roberta Bondi puts it.

Our parents do stand as God-substitutes, or divine signposts at least, in our early years, for they lay the foundations on which we build our own self-understanding and self-acceptance. However, it is in relationship to God alone that we can truly find our identity, which is why our seeing of God can have such profound healing effects on us. It lifts us out of introspection to focus on the Other who is truly Centre of all that is. In the very act of doing so, we find ourselves. This is well expressed in a book on worship by three authors who say:

Worship is enjoying God. In worship our attention is directed away from ourselves, to

God and to our neighbour. We do not 'enjoy
ourselves' in worship, indeed the very opposite; at the start we look at ourselves honestly
and confess our sins, then as forgiven sinners
we can cease to be absorbed by self and open
out to God and his glory, and our neighbour
and his needs.

Sin, according to a phrase much used by
Augustine and Luther, means being *incurvatus
in se*, turning in on self. C.S. Lewis found an
amazing release from this obsession with self
when he was given the capacity of enjoying
God and consequently his neighbour.
(Forrester/McDonald/Tellini, *Encounter with
God* [T&T. Clark, Edinburgh. '83] p. 5)

Lost or found?

The parable of the prodigal son is the story of
someone making a journey of discovery about
their true identity and 'home'. It has a particular
relevance to modern Western culture.

The journey begins through seeking independence from all relationships—the cry for freedom.
But although the gift of freedom is given by
the Father, the discovery of the true self is not
found. The prodigal is adrift on a chartless sea of
experiences in relationships which give no identity
or meaning. So too for us, we are in an uncharted
sea of individuality in which no authority or
relationship beyond the self can have a shaping
significance. It is not surprising that loneliness

is such a major sickness of our culture. Included in this search is a seeking of identity through wealth—dividing the property. It seems to give some identity, or rather it buys some time and some 'friendship', but it neither satisfies, lasts, nor delivers what it promised. The identity sought in wealth leads into identity sought in relationships—riotous living, so the elder brother informs us. Here again, there is no answer to the cry 'tell me who I am'.

The money dries up, the friends disappear, and the end seems at hand. But truly it is the beginning, for he 'comes to his senses' and starts the journey home to the One who can give him identity, meaning, significance and self-worth.

The welcome he receives gives him the identity he sought. 'This my son', says it all. The words are then reinforced by the outward symbols of celebration and affirmation, namely the robe of sonship, the sandals of a freeman, and the ring of authority. Now he knows who he is. He has found himself in discovering the One whose service is perfect freedom.

It is a journey we all need to make; out of the hell of self-centredness into liberation to know and be known by God, and consequently by ourselves and by others.

Breakthrough

Writing those words puts me immediately in touch with a particular crisis moment in my late teenage years. I retain a vivid awareness of the experience. It was a Sunday afternoon, and I had a deep and

distressing sense of non-being, of not knowing who
I was, or in what way I could 'find myself'—not
that I could have put it in such words at the time.
All I knew was that unless help was found soon I
was heading for a nervous breakdown—that day.

That afternoon God graciously intervened
through my reading Paul Tournier's book, *The
Meaning of Persons*. I was nearing the end of the
book when the sentence leapt out of the page at me
as a lifeline to a drowning person, or a signpost to
a tired and lost traveller.

> To depend on God is to be free of men, things
> and self. It is to be able to take pleasure in
> all his gifts without being the slave of any. It
> is to be able, as occasion demands, to spend
> and to save, to speak and to forbear, to act
> and to rest, to be grave and gay, to defend
> oneself and to surrender.
> (Paul Tournier, *The Meaning of Persons*, p. 228)

The sense of relief brought me to tears, to sanity
and to joy. It was pure gift of healing truth.

Conversion

It is for this reason that I have used the word
conversion as the theological term for 'knowing'.
It is about turning round to face Another, and
so finding our identity through a new and outer-
directed awareness of God. It is a Copernican revo-
lution; seeing Another as Centre of all that is.

The picture that I have found helpful is that of

the guidance system used for spacecraft. Because everything in space is moving, the earth, planets, sun, moon and stars, it is not possible to send a command to 'Go one hundred miles an hour faster', for the question is 'faster than what?' So what happens is that the craft is 'locked on' to a distant star, which is so far away that for all practical purposes it is a 'fixed' star. Then, all commands sent to the spacecraft can be sent in terms of that fixed point. You can direct the craft to go faster towards, or from, or at a prescribed angle in relation to, that fixed point. And that is the nature of our relationship to God. He is the one by whom we steer our way through life. It is in relation to him that we live out our lives.

But the best is yet to come. Once we are locked on to God, we discover that he is in active communication with us, for he is the One who has revealed himself both as Love and Word. The Cross underlines that such a Being is quite literally 'dying to communicate with us'. Our Star is a speaking, loving, living, fixed point. Which means we need a good receiver to accept the messages that are communicated to us. It is in this that we discover our identity and find a self to do the loving which God has called us into.

Prayer as receiving

If we need a self to 'do the loving', then prayer will involve learning to receive. This sometimes makes for difficulty for modern people. We are more at home with prayer as achieving, getting, doing, and working; even prayer as authenticating us as 'good Christians'. Prayer as receiving is

comparatively unknown territory. It also touches
on our allergy which we looked at in chapter one.
Receiving in prayer may seem strange, and feel
like hard work. But it is vital that we do this
work, and break through the fear of being on the
receiving end of love.

But how?

Essentially we do this as we learn to receive
God's words of love and affirmation addressed to
us. Here we run into a real barrier—our double
standards. We think it thoroughly 'Christian'
to affirm others, to tell them they matter to
God, that they are good people, pleasing to God
and us. But we cannot accept that of ourselves.
Equally, what we find acceptable to say about
ourselves ('I'm stupid', 'I'm no good', 'I always
get it wrong', 'I'm useless'), we think would be
thoroughly un-Christian to say, or even think,
about someone else.

In other words we can celebrate another's humanity, but not our own. Which is where we need to
begin, for *we are made in the image of God*. That
is the starting point of scripture and should be
the starting point of our own self-acceptance. We
matter to God, we are made to reflect his likeness
(his personality, his ability to think, to create,
to choose and to love), and to participate in his
work of creation. That 'creative work' may be in
building a factory, making music, or a family, a
school or a business. It may express itself in
relationships, in 'making a case' for some political
issue, or simply in bringing about harmony and
peace among the people whose lives we touch.

Celebrating the fact that we are made in the
image of God is the beginning of our journey into
wholeness. The next step is to receive, and rejoice

in, the fact that *God has set his love on us through Christ.*

A story to ponder

The annunciation by Gabriel to Mary is an icon, or type, of the whole church. The angel addresses Mary with the words 'Greetings, you who are highly favoured!' (Lk 1:28). 'Hail Mary, full of grace' does not do justice to the words. The greeting is not about what she is, in her own right and by her own efforts, it is about who she has become because the grace, goodness, and love of God are upon her.

PRAYER OF THE HEART:
Affirming the image of God in us.

Almighty God,
who wonderfully created us in your own
*   image*
and yet more wonderfully restored us in
*   your Son Jesus Christ:*
grant that, as he came to share our human
*   nature,*
so we may be partakers of his divine glory:
who is alive and reigns with you and the
*   Holy Spirit,*
one God, now and for ever. Amen.
(ASB Collect for the first Sunday after
    Christmas)

Mary is a symbol of the whole church. Like her we are chosen, loved and filled with grace, by the goodness and mercy of God. Like her, the Spirit overshadows us so that Christ can be 'born afresh in us' (Gal 4:19). Like her, we are to respond in obedience and faith, or rather with the faith that produces the fruit of freely chosen obedience.

So we can see ourselves, like Mary, favoured by God's love. Like her we need to ponder them in our heart and nourish our soul on the goodness of such love. We need to receive before we have anything to give.

The cycle of grace

Frank Lake, one of the first people to seek to integrate psychological insights with the Christian faith, developed what he called the 'cycle of grace'. By this he meant the way that life is intended to flow. He identified four stages.

First we are to experience *acceptance*, simply for being who we are. If that is a regular part of our experience of life we experience *sustenance* because we are valued. It is that which gives us our *significance*. Because we matter to others, and to God. Out of that grows our ability to make valued *achievements* in life.

That is very helpful. Yet the most helpful thing is what Frank Lake also said, namely that our unredeemed nature tends to flow the other way round. We try to *achieve* things, so that they will give us *significance*, which will *sustain* us, and enable us to *accept* ourselves. The trouble is that life will not flow that way round.

In the old vicarage we used to live in, the central heating system had been added to over the years, Heath Robinson style. The result was that sometimes the water went the wrong way round. When that happened the pump could not work and the whole system was dependent on gravity. The hot water went in at the bottom of the cylinder, and came out tepid. It is a picture of what happens when we do not begin our relationship with God on the basis of our acceptance in Christ.

Once we do so, grace can flow. Then we can celebrate our existence, and move on to celebrate God's and the whole of creation. Rather than making us self-centred, such experience of personal worth gives us the security with which to step into the suffering of the world.

This is the good news of the gospel applied to our inner being. We need to apply it regularly to ourselves if we are to live life to the full, by grace rather than law. It is this dynamic that is expressed in the prayer exercise which follows.

Affirming the true self

All too easily Christians take a negative view of life, and of the self. After all, does not scripture teach us to crucify the old self? Leanne Payne has written so well on this subject that I want to give her answer at this point:

> The soul, with its new centre in Christ, radically changed and redirected, is to be accepted. There is the oddest thing about the history of Christian teaching. This new, real self is largely ignored, feared, or even denied. If one doubts this, he need simply run through the references in the best Bible helps. There the old or false self is

catalogued and referenced in every possible
way, which is absolutely good and necessary.
But where is the real self acknowledged? It
goes largely uncelebrated, unreferenced, and
in effect unaccepted ... Until this redeemed
self is acknowledged and accepted, we live
out of the immature, unaffirmed self, and we
cannot hear God aright ... Until we accept
the new self, we are dangerous to ourselves
and to others.

(Leanne Payne, *The Healing Presence*
[Kingsway Publications, Eastbourne. '89] p.48)

Is this not at the root of the allergy and folly
which, as we saw in the first chapter, keeps us
from prayer? We fear that we will be 'found out' by
coming that close to God. Yet he comes to give life
to the true self, to release the riches of his image in
us. He comes to give love, and affirm our worth. If
our prayer is not touched by this magnetic power
of love, which draws us in, we have not yet become
properly attuned to God.

This is the joyful evidence of growth in prayer—
the enjoyment of God, and the personal sense of
being and well-being which we receive in the
process of encounter with him. It is about this
that our prayer exercise is concerned. However,
there is a further prayer principle to spell out,
which can be of great help to us in setting the
truth of God's love for us deep in our hearts.

Affirmation as prayer

There is too much asking in prayer. Especially
asking for what is already ours. One way to break

out of this pattern is to learn the art and place of affirmation as a way of praying.

PRAYER PRINCIPLE FOUR
AFFIRMATION NOURISHES FAITH
God has promised us much, and given us all things richly to enjoy.
We do not have to ask for his generosity, love and blessing—but receive them.
We do that best by turning our prayers into positive affirmations of the truth.

Imagine waiting in a room to be interviewed for a new post which you are eager to get. Sitting there you are likely to be nervous. As a Christian, it is natural to turn to prayer. However, what we are likely to do is use our emotional energy to fuel prayer—but in a negative way. So we will pray something like 'Lord, help me not to be anxious', 'Help me not to make a fool of myself', 'Please give me your peace.' Valid, at one level, though each of these prayers is, what they are doing is underlining a negative in us. They are stating, in turn, that we are anxious, likely to make a fool of ourselves, and lacking peace. Yet, God has told us that he loves us, will be with us to the close of the Age, and is in us.

To pray by affirmation in that situation, we simply turn the prayers into statements of the truth. 'Thank you for your peace', 'I receive your wisdom for this interview', 'Thank you that you are with me, you are my strength', 'You are Lord of my future—my times are in your hands'. In this way we use our prayer to express, and so build, faith. One such affirmation we taught the whole church in my last job was:

In the multitude of Your mercies,
the greatness of Your grace,
and the power of Your Presence,
we are being made whole,
in the likeness of Christ.

Many found it a great blessing, and an aid to
faith—which is what prayer is meant to be. And
that is particularly so when it comes to entering
into God's acceptance of us. If we spend time
praying 'Lord, help me to accept myself, we are
not likely to make progress. Such a prayer is
underlining to our inner being that we do not
accept ourselves. Giving thanks, and acting on
the truth of scripture is a richer way to pray.

Especially is the principle of the prayer of affirmation helpful when it is linked to the principle
we looked at earlier of developing a liturgy of the
heart. For the fact is that what we say regularly
and build into our unconscious and subconscious
has a powerful and formative effect on us. It
shapes our thinking, behaviour and belief.

PRAYER EXERCISE: Receiving
the good news into our hearts

Sit down and get yourself in a comfortable position.
Seek to be still, remaining silent for a minute
   or two.
Move towards focusing on God.
– through slow repeating of the two words 'Our
   Father',
– or the words of a well-known song or hymn,
– the use of an icon, or lighted candle,

– or you might like to have a picture of a beautiful
  plant or great tree, (which you can use to remind
  yourself that good things take time to grow).
Let these means aid your faith in God's presence
  and his love towards you.

Remember and rejoice before God that

> The Spirit helps us in our weakness. We do
> not know what we ought to pray for, but the
> Spirit himself intercedes for us with groans
> that words cannot express. (Rom 8:26)

Now ask God to give you good things to say to
yourself which come from him.

Here are a number of things that we can all say
to ourselves, repeat them slowly to yourself a
number of times.
If they stir any response in you speak that out,
If not, simply keep repeating one of these truths.

I recommend that you decide beforehand how long
to do it for (say five or ten minutes) and keep to
that time.
This way you undermine any instinct to put yourself down for 'not doing it for longer'.
In any case the more important thing is doing
it regularly (preferably several times a week for
several weeks).
Remember, truth takes time to become rooted and
to grow in us.

While you may well find it helpful to start with
one of the sentences below, my encouragement
to you is to expect that God will give *you* just

the right words to speak into your heart. When
that happens, rejoice—and forget my suggestions!
However, here are some truths that you can speak
into your inner being:

> The God who made the universe, celebrates
>   my existence. (Alleluia)
> I matter to God.
> I am chosen and loved in Christ.
> I am accepted in the Beloved.

Yes, because we are baptised 'into Christ' we can
even say God's Word to us

> You are my child whom I love; with you I am
> well pleased

Remember that children, for their health, need
affirmation about their essential worth and goodness. As children of God we also need affirmation.
We have a part to play in the work of evangelism
—by evangelising (that is, proclaiming good news)
to ourselves.

Chapter 6

Good Grief!
Encountering God through Weakness

*Prayer connects us with ourselves; it is the
link between our new selves that are always
being transformed into God's image and
our old selves with which we must come to
terms if we are to be transformed.*
Roberta Bondi, *To Pray and to Love*, p. 12

*Healthy shame is the psychological
foundation of humility. It is the source of
spirituality.*
John Bradshaw, *Healing the shame
that binds you*, p. vii

Prayer is the application of the *good news* to
the human heart. That is the work which was
addressed in the last chapter. But there is another
side, the dark side of human nature and experience. That also needs to be addressed in prayer.
We cannot begin to address it until we have 'a
self to do the loving'. But when we are secure in
that Love, we know we can face the truth and not
be overwhelmed or destroyed. Which is why we
considered the receiving of God's love first. Now,

however, we can consider the other side, and know
that we will not be rejected.

Too much prayer by Christians begins, continues and ends, in guilt. That is so tragic, for
conversion is about turning from darkness to face
and enter and enjoy (be enjoined to) the Light
of Christ. The gospel is about liberation from
guilt, not living in it. Moreover, not all of the
darkness we need to face, by any means, is our
responsibility, our sin. The grief we often have to
face is from the wounds we have received.

Our coming to God in this area ought not to be
too difficult. Many of us first encountered God in
the darkness. That darkness includes the wounds
we have experienced in life, the stubborn questions that refuse to yield up answers, the hostility
and injustice we experience from time to time, as
well as the hostility and injustice we perpetrate
on others.

How do we handle such painful issues in prayer?
Essentially, it is a matter of learning to grieve well.
To be in touch with our anger that results from our
experience of loss, to yield to the sorrow by letting
go of what is no longer an option, and then to find
God's way of transcending the loss by seeing it
transfigured in God's purposes. That transfiguring
through faith that we are led into sometimes is the
strength to live with unanswered questions and
know that God is there. We turn now to consider
several different aspects of such good grief.

Catching the little foxes

In the work of farming vineyards, the children
of Israel had particular problems with the little

foxes. The adult ones would eat the grapes. It was frustrating, but not distressing. There were a limited number of grapes a fox could reach. It was the little foxes which had a more devastating effect, for in early spring they would eat the growing shoots of that year's branches. If the growing shoots were destroyed, the whole crop was lost, for there would be no vine on which a crop could grow. It is this trouble which forms the backdrop to the prayer of the Lover:

Catch for us the foxes,
the little foxes
that ruin the vineyards,
our vineyards that are in bloom.
(Song of Songs 2:15)

Notice that it is the Lover (God) addressing the Beloved (Israel). There is a vital job to do, without which there can be no fruit of intimacy between them (see John 15). It is the work of protecting the growth at its first beginnings.

For us the little foxes in our experience are the inner attitudes which eat away at the Divine affirmation of the true self which the gospel brings to us, which we considered in the last chapter. All too quickly the new shoots of self-acceptance and self-worth can be destroyed. Our task is to catch those little put downs, those negative thought patterns, that would rob us of the fruit of the gospel in our lives.

We can do this best by listening to our inner dialogue and turning it up to God in prayer, seeking from him new ways of seeing ourselves and addressing our inner heart. This is no easy

task for that inner dialogue has often become so
entrenched that it is a quite unconscious process
going on within us, and shaping the way in which
we view ourselves and the world. We may never
say to ourselves 'I'm no good', 'I don't matter': but
our lifestyle shouts it from the rooftops. Those are
the little foxes we must catch.

When we have caught them, we need to bring
them before God and ask him to give us words that
bring life. We need to replace the inner attitude
of 'I don't matter', by some verse from scripture
such as:

> The Lord your God is with you,
>   he is mighty to save.
> He will take great delight in you,
>   he will quiet you with his love,
>   he will rejoice over you with singing.
>   (Zeph 3:17)

Indeed it is good to personalise such scriptures,
and turn then into affirmations, by repeating to
our hearts the truth that 'God is with me, he is
mighty to save'. 'He takes delight in . . .' This
work of catching the little foxes is part of listening
prayer. It is something that needs to take place
continually.

Dealing with the wounds of the past (and present)

The little foxes of our inner dialogue usually gain
entrance to our souls through wounds from deep
in our past. In particular, they come from a lack

of full love and affirmation from our parents
or 'primary care-givers'. We experienced love as
conditional, not a gift prior to our existence, but
a gift dependent on our proper performing. That
proper performing may be about outward achievements which would reflect well on others, or a
more inward performance of giving the emotional
response that meets the needs of those on whose
love we know ourselves to be total dependent.

Dealing with these wounds involves becoming
free from parental control and their image and
expectations of us. It is no easy step, masked
so often by protestations of having had a happy
childhood. It may have been happy, apart from
the issue that needs dealing with. Equally, what
happened (good or bad) may have been described
to us as 'good', and we have imbibed a lie, which
has shaped our view of God, life and ourselves.
Concerning these wounds, Leanne Payne writes:

> Until this redeemed self is acknowledged
> and accepted, we live out of the immature,
> unaffirmed self, and we cannot hear God
> aright. From that centre, we also 'mishear'
> our fellows, and they become the target of the
> diseased 'matter' that yet resides within our
> souls—that is, our fear of rejection, our bit-
> terness, envy, anger and sense of inferiority.
> These invariably project themselves into the
> minds and hearts of those we love the most,
> piercing them like deadly arrows.
> (Leanne Payne, *The Healing Presence*
> [Kingsway Publications, Eastbourne. '89] p. 48)

Though we can benefit from the skilled counsel
of others, there is much we can do for ourselves.

Remember, it is the Lover who tells the Beloved
to catch the little foxes. The prayer exercise at the
end of this chapter can be of great help in enabling
us to 'name' and root out wounds from the past. It
involves calling sin by its name, and recognising
that we have been sinned against. We can then
release that wound to the Wounded One on the
Cross. Then we complete the work by releasing
anyone who put that wound upon us. We do that
as we speak out forgiveness of them, before God,
releasing them from the debt they owe us (Matt
18:32–33).

This is doing the work of grieving, entering
into the loss of our wholeness, and the pain
experienced with close relationships. It is a good
work that leads to life.

Making a good confession

We would be foolish indeed to think that all our
trials are somehow 'their fault'. That very attitude
of abdicating responsibility is a refusal to accept
our responsibility for the sin that swirls around
our suffering world. We need not only to learn to
accept ourselves, and to forgive others, but also to
confess our sins.

As I said at the beginning of this chapter, too
much prayer by Christians begins, continues and
ends in guilt. The tragedy is that we do not break
free at the end. We rise from prayer no less guilty,
but marginally more conscious of sinfulness. We
fail to enter into what Paul described as the
'glorious freedom of the children of God' (Rom
8:21). Our problem is often in discovering how to
do that. Problems surface at two points, discerning

true guilt and discovering true forgiveness. Let us
explore these two matters further.

The first problem is that of *discerning true guilt*.
The Psalmist himself knew the problem: 'who can
discern his errors?' (Ps 19:12). Remember there
are several sources of 'accusation' against us.
Other people can say 'the trouble with you is . . .'
or 'You are unloving . . .' We also accuse ourselves
to our own hearts. The devil is described as the
'accuser of our brothers, who accuses them before
our God day and night' (Rev 12:10). Indeed we
know he seems especially active at night. The devil
works overtime. God also accuses us, bringing us
to awareness of true guilt.

The best way of discerning true guilt is to look
up—to God—not in on self. The Psalmist prays:

> Search me, O God, and know my heart;
>   test me and know my anxious thoughts
> See if there is any offensive way in me,
>   and lead me in the way everlasting.
>   (Ps 139:23–24)

Notice that he does not do the searching, he leaves
that to God. He seems to work on the principle of
'innocent until proved guilty'. Part of our diseased
heart is that we presume ourselves to be always
guilty.

My experience is that false guilt is a vague
feeling of being bad, rather than having done
wrong, and that it makes me trapped, depressed,
unable or disinclined to take any steps. True guilt,
by contrast, comes often as a shaft of light. It is
frequently attached to the 'way everlasting'. In
other words I see the way I should be going, I
receive vision about right living, and that makes

me aware of 'where I have gone wrong'. It is no
great effort then to change, for I have 'seen the
light'. True guilt, when joined to the work of
Christ on the Cross, liberates *into* not just *from*.
Watching for the *'intos'* is one of the best ways of
seeing sin.

The next step is owning sin. From the Garden
of Eden onwards, we have been incredible blame-
shifters. But it does not work. We cannot be rid
of something which we do not admit is ours. We
have to own it. Naming our sins is as vital, and
life giving, as naming our blessings. We name
our blessings in order to get hold of them more
firmly. We name our sins in order to let go of
them completely. So we name what is wrong, give
it to God, and see him taking it into himself on the
Cross.

The other thing we need to do is that of *discovering true forgiveness*. Jesus was in no doubt that
celebration was the end result of recovering the
lost, as the parables of the lost coin, the lost sheep,
and the prodigal son make clear (Lk 15). There
is celebration in each one. The angels in heaven
celebrate. The woman and the shepherd celebrate.
The prodigious father celebrates in no uncertain
fashion. I have found it important, in confession,
always to make a double confession. Whenever
I confess my sins, I conclude by confessing *also*
that Jesus is my Saviour from sin. This is self-
administered absolution. You do not have to be
ordained to do it; the only qualification is being
someone who owns their sins.

Owning idols and addictions

There is one further area in dealing with sin
that we need to pay attention to. All too easily

we see sin as 'sins', specific wrong actions we
have done such as being cruel or dishonest. But
sin is deeper than sins. Sins are what we do.
Sin is what has us. So there is an important
work of recognising the things that control us
and drive us. The remarkable work of Alcoholics
Anonymous has arisen out of the courage to do just
that. The first step in the 'twelve step recovery
programme' is:

> 'We admitted we were powerless over (what-
> ever addiction) and our lives had become
> unmanageable.'
> (Quoted from, John Bradshaw, *Healing the
> Shame That Binds You* [Health communica-
> tions, Florida. '88] p.125)

Listening to God to bring us face to face with our
idols and addictions, is a very important part of
both confession (of sin, rather than sins), and of
the work of grieving. Without it we will not be
free. We will be driven people. Driven by we know
not what.

Addictions are not simply those associated with
chemical dependence (drugs and alcohol). An addiction is anything around which I have so organised
my life that it now runs and controls me. There
are 'process addictions', such as the need to keep
the peace, to keep everyone happy, as well as
workaholics and those who are addicted to hob-
bies in an all-consuming way. There are also
relationship addictions, 'love addictions' as Pia
Mellody—the author of *Facing Love Addictions*
(Harper, San Francisco '92)—calls it.

The biblical term for addictions is idols. Luke
Johnson's definition of an idol is something I

frequently come back to in my own prayer and
meditation, in order to allow God to clear out any
false goals and objects of 'undue attention' in my
life. He says:

> My god is that which
> rivets my attention,
> centres my activity,
> preoccupies my mind,
> and motivates my action.
>
> (Luke T. Johnson, *Sharing Possessions*
> [SCM Press, London. '81] p.49)

Put more simply still, if you watch where your
mind wanders to, when it wanders, you may well
catch an idol lurking in the undergrowth of your
inner life. Again, we become free of such idols
when we own we have them (or rather that they
have us), bring them before God, renounce them,
and receive the gift of forgiveness and liberation.

Global grief

Being in touch with personal grief, vulnerability
and sin, makes us aware of the greater reservoir
of human and global pain and injustice. Once that
happens we are in a position to use that in our
intercession for the world. That takes us into the
final stage of grief work, namely, transcendence.
Transcendence involves handling the pain in such
a way that we, and the world around us, are
enriched by the experience. This happens for
example in bereavement when we incorporate
into ourselves the values and characteristics of
the person whose death we mourn. They live on

in us. It happens through forgiveness, when we release others from bondage of being our debtor; we incorporate something of the heart of God by the practice of forgiveness. In this stage we are able to use the pain and brokenness of human existence to grow in our humanity and the work of compassion.

Jill Saward, the 'Ealing vicarage rape victim' is a fine example of someone who has experienced brutal treatment and worked through the grief to a place of transcending that pain. She has recently formed an organisation to help other rape victims. Here is the fruit of grief that can overcome evil with good.

George Hoffman, the founder of TEAR Fund—an evangelical relief agency—once said at a meeting I attended that 'two thirds of those who have gone out to work on development projects in the third world, are motivated by anger'. This was in no way a criticism, but rather a positive reporting. For anger can be positive energy that motivates action. Here are people in touch with the suffering of the world, who themselves are deeply touched by the injustice of the situation and are motivated to 'do something about it'. Awareness of the injustices in the world is transformed into compassionate action.

PRAYER OF THE HEART:
The cry for help

O Lord, listen!
O Lord, forgive!
O Lord, hear and act!
For your sake, O my God, do not delay.
(Dan 9:19)

Such transcendence begins most healthily in prayer, but will not stop when we rise from our knees. Indeed it will direct the way we walk thereafter. So prayer and life are woven together if we are properly engaged in the work of grieving.

It is worth pointing out that here we are already in the realm of intercession and in the area of *going* rather than *knowing*. However, I raise these issues now because they do surface when we are in touch with our own grief. Moreover, I want to underline the fact that the three aspects of encountering God which form the framework of the book (namely, *seeing, knowing* and *going*) have soft-focus boundaries. They flow into, and out of, each other. It would be a perversion of what I am seeking to communicate to take this framework as any sort of straitjacket or technique. They are simply three aspects that are woven together in life ad in prayer.

Being and groaning

In Romans chapter eight, we see the process of the previous two chapters—coming into a secure sense of being, and being in touch with and working through grief—expounded in a marvellous way. First, Paul affirms the true self that emerges out of relationship to God in Christ, by the Spirit when he writes:

> For you did not receive a spirit that makes you a slave again to fear, but you received the Spirit of sonship. And by him we cry, 'Abba, Father.' The Spirit himself testifies with our spirit that we are God's children.
>
> (Rom 8:15–16)

Here is the believers' security of relationship, and sense of self-worth, which enables them to face and be in touch with pain and loss. He then goes on to speak of a threefold grieving that touches the individual, reaches out to the whole created order, and comes from the heart of God himself.

> We know that the whole creation has been groaning as in the pains of childbirth right up to the present time. Not only so, but we ourselves, who have the firstfruits of the Spirit, groan inwardly as we wait eagerly for our adoption . . . the Spirit himself intercedes for us with groans that words cannot express.
>
> (Rom 8:22, 23, 26.)

So the true work of grief does not turn us in on ourselves, but leads us out into the suffering of the world; as Dietrich Bonhoeffer put it, 'A Christian is someone who shares the sufferings of God in the world.' We will return to this again when we consider the work of intercession.

Learning not to fear the dark

In all these ways, as we face our own human frailty and that of others, we can learn to handle these experiences in a way which is life giving. When we do that we receive a bonus—the ability to encounter God and grow as people, through facing the darkness. Indeed we come to associate difficulties, trials and testing as doors into life.

Jacob wrestling with an angel 'until the dawn' becomes a symbol of hope for all of us wrestling with unknown forces in dark places in our lives. It is the place where growth takes place, which

is why the wilderness is a symbol for encounter
with God. As one of the characters in John Wyatt's
book, *The Shining Levels*, says:

> You Europeans are obsessed with Things.
> You no longer know the meaning of simplic-
> ity. And as truth is pure simplicity you can
> hardly recognise it. To find truth you need
> to give up every Thing. Truth is brought to
> the world by lonely men living simply in the
> wilderness.
>   (John Wyatt, *The Shining Levels*
>   [Fontana] p. 45)

Character is formed in the dark. The Beatitudes
point us to this truth. They begin at the place of
pain, failure and vulnerability—blessed are the
poor in spirit, and blessed are those who mourn,
being the first two. But they end in strength.
The strength to become peacemakers, co-creators
of harmony with God; this is not peacekeeping,
but a richer, stronger, making of something whole
which did not previously exist. They end with the
strength to withstand the assaults of a hostile
world—'Blessed are those who are persecuted for
my name's sake.' Such strength is a vulnerable,
yet powerful and healing, strength. It does not
control or dictate; rather it gives and it liberates. It
is this holy strength of character which God gives
to those with the courage and will to practise these
varied aspects of good grieving.

PRAYER EXERCISE: The garden of the heart

This exercise brings together the last two chapters, dealing with the affirmation of love that

comes from God, and the help to face the darkness
within. I am indebted to Leanne Payne for this
prayer exercise, the first part of which she uses
to good effect in her Prayer Counselling Ministry
Conferences. The second part is the natural, and
balancing, progression.

Preparation

See your life as a garden, in which there are weeds
that need to be dug up.
Be still, and take time to enter this garden; enjoy
the sunlight and fragrance of its flowers.
– get in touch with its size, its layout, and the
  emotions of being in it.

Weeding

See the weeds, and seek to get them out by the
roots.
You will need the help of the Gardener to do a
thorough and skilled job
– remember, Mary supposed that that was what
  he was (Jn 20:15).
Let him show you your part—trust him with
his part.

Take time to do a thorough job.
See if you can name the weed(s) that needs to be
  removed.
– seek his help if you need help in naming the
  issue.

Notice what is done with the weeds after they are
removed.
Reflect on the experience (do not rush it, or step
too quickly out of it into 'analysis'),

– what does the experience tell you about what
  God wants to root out of your life?
– note your response to this weeding; is it eager,
  anxious, relieved, or what?
  Note any way that it speaks to you: put it down
  in your prayer journal.

Planting

Now comes the planting of new plants for future
flowering.
('love, joy, peace, like flowers, spring in his path
to birth')
– enjoy this good experience.
Imagine the pleasure and peace and enjoyment of
filling the garden with colour.
– notice the smallest plants (the alpines) and the
  sturdy bushes: they all have a place.
– notice what is there: you are not starting from
  scratch. Good plants already bloom there.

Be aware of the ways you and the Gardener are
working together.
Name the plants—what do they symbolise in
your life?
– ask for help in naming the plants if you need
  it.
– stand back and enjoy what has been planted;
  imagine the growth in one or two months or one
  or two years' time. Enjoy it with him.

What does the experience tell you that God is
wanting to plant in your life?
– make a note of every aspect of the experience
  which speaks to you.

Chapter 7

Praying Back the Scriptures
Encountering God through
Bible Meditation

*The word of God is a special sacrament of
his presence, just as real, although different
in form, as his presence in the Eucharist.*
Gerard Hughes, *God of Surprises* (Darton,
Longman and Todd, London '85) p.46

*The first principle in beginning to listen to
God is that of taking the sacred texts into
our very spirits and souls by prayerful
meditation upon them.*
*His word then 'abides is us', burning as an
inner light, and we cry out to God.*
*This is oratio, responsive speech born of
God's word aflame within.*
Leanne Payne, *The Broken Image* (Kingsway
Publications, Eastbourne, '81) p.146

Notwithstanding Thomas Cranmer's masterly
crafting of the Church of England's Book
of Common Prayer—and the work in our own
day of the Liturgical Commission of the Church
of England—the Bible is *the* Christian's Prayer

Book. It is our greatest source of prayer and our great resource in praying.

Indeed prayer and scripture are rather like the oxygen and hydrogen which, when mixed together, ignite and create 'lift off' for the space shuttle and other rockets. The power of these two forces, in our case of prayer and the reading of scripture, can truly lift us into the heavens. Too often Christians have these two resources in seperate sealed containers with no means of mixing.

This chapter is about 'mixing it' in prayer! It is about how to harness the power of God's Word to our prayer life. The mixing is not just of scripture and our prayers, but of scripture and our lives. Prayer is simply the mixer, the means of joining life and truth. How does it happen?

Our knowing of God comes to us in large measure through our encounter with him in meditation on scripture. God's Word is creative energy. By a word God created the whole universe. By his living Word, Jesus Christ, he has redeemed the whole of that creation, bringing it back within his eternal purposes. He now comes to us, between creation and the consummation of the ages, to continue his work in the process of new creation within and through the believer. God does so by speaking his Word into our lives, to bring his likeness into being and to give us a foretaste of the fulfilment to come.

Truly to hear, and in listening to obey, is at the heart of knowing God.

That knowing is itself a gift of God. It points to the double source of the inspiration of scripture. God not only breathed life and truth into those who wrote, by which they become a living word to us, but he now breathes life into the hearers of his Word, by which we become alive with the truth of God.

I had a striking experience of this on the very first day of my being a Christian. After making a commitment to Christ on Easter Eve, as a teenager, I went to bed thinking the whole thing had been a waste of time. I felt no different. Yet, the next morning, the whole world seemed different. Easter Day really was 'a passover of gladness, a passover of God'.

In the afternoon, the person who had brought me to faith spent half an hour showing me verses in the Bible which explained what it means to be a Christian and to live by faith in God. Until the day before, I had rated the Bible the most boring book in the world—well actually, it was equally top (or bottom?!) with Shakespeare. However, that day it came alive to me, and spoke as if it were personally addressed only to me. This was no longer a school textbook. It was more like a love letter; intimate, affirming, understanding, and speaking with deep empathy into my experience of life.

True knowing

This knowing and being known takes place when God's Word so penetrates our innermost being that we become what we hear. We are transformed into God's likeness. This is the encounter with God which is the glory of the New Covenant, as Paul wrote of it:

> Whenever anyone turns to the Lord, the veil is taken away. Now the Lord is the Spirit, and where the Spirit of the Lord is, there is freedom. And we, who with unveiled faces all reflect the Lord's glory, are being transformed into his likeness with ever-increasing

glory, which comes from the Lord, who is the
Spirit. (2 Cor 3:16–18)

The importance of listening as the key to *knowing*
is underlined by Old and New Testaments alike.
The listening that is meant here is a deep hearing
of the inner heart which is transformed by that
hearing. This is how intimacy with God takes
place. We know by hearing. Significantly it was
the lack of true hearing which was God's chief
complaint against the false prophets:

> If they had stood in my council,
>   they would have proclaimed my words to
>   my people
> and would have turned them from their evil
>   ways and from their evil desires.
>
>   (Jer 23:22)

The contrast with the Servant of the Lord, in
Isaiah, is striking. Of him we read:

> The Sovereign Lord has given me an
>   instructed tongue, to know the word that
>   sustains the weary.
> He wakens me morning by morning,
>   wakens my ear to listen like one being
>   taught.
> The Sovereign Lord has opened my ears,
>   and I have not been rebellious.
>
>   (Is 50:4–5)

Jesus continually urged his disciples to listen at
this level with the whole of their being: 'He
who has ears to hear, let him hear' (Matt 11:15;
13:9–17; 13:43). How then can we listen 'with our

whole heart' so that we may be transformed from
one degree of glory to another? For this is the purpose of our knowing and being known by God.

Personal dialogue

The key to such prayer lies in establishing a dialogue between ourselves and God. One particular
principle has been vital in my own experience of
prayer. It is a principle we will be returning to
repeatedly in the remaining chapters of the book.

It is encapsulated in the, at first sight, puzzling
phrase 'liturgical sentence and charismatic response'. That may not be enlightening by itself, so
let me explain. What I mean is that there is both
a set ('fixed') part of prayer, and a spontaneous
('free') part. It is an enormous help in our prayer
life if we can develop a rhythm of speaking out
a 'liturgical sentence' (a set verse of scripture or
part of a hymn or prayer), and then express our
own response in our own words (that is what I
mean by 'charismatic response').

PRAYER PRINCIPLE FIVE
SENTENCE AND RESPONSE STRUCTURE
*Using a set text, whether scripture, poetry,
hymn or prayer, and making our own
spontaneous response as an expression of
prayer liberates us from undue responsibility
for prayer being wholly dependent on us.*

So, for example, we can use a well-known verse
such as 'God so loved the world . . .', and, as we
meditate on it, we make response to God. We

thank him that he does love the world, or we can ask him to enable us to love the world as Jesus did, or pray that the world he has made will discover and experience that love.

This a very simple, easy to remember, way of meditating on scripture. Moreover it applies to practically the whole of scripture. Almost Any verse can draw out of us a response of prayer or worship. All we need to do is to read a phrase, sentence or verse from scripture and then respond to God from within that verse.

At the end of this chapter is an exercise designed to help us take God's Word into our lives in this way. It is an approach which Colin Urquhart develops throughout the whole of his book *In Christ Jesus*, and outlines particularly on page 93.

The seed of the Word

The purpose of praying back the scriptures is to take them to heart. That is, to take them into our heart, our innermost nature, so that we are shaped by what we hear. The cynic has said of humanity that 'we are what we eat'. The Christian, feeding alike on God's Word and the sacrament of communion, can say 'Amen' to that—not out of cynicism, but by faith.

The harvest analogy, seen most clearly in the parable of the Sower, expresses this truth about the seed of God's Word being planted in our lives. It tells us that 'the one who sowed the good seed is the Son of Man' (Matt 13:37). God's word is like a seed planted in us which is to grow to maturity (1 Pet 1:23–25). Praying back the scriptures is the way both to plant and to water

that seed (Is 61:3) The same imagery lies behind
the picture of the Vine and the branches in John
chapter 15.

This way of handling scripture is far from new.
It is part of the history of spiritual life in all
the traditions of the church. The importance of
'hiding God's word in our heart' (Ps 119:11) is
rooted first of all in scripture itself. Joshua is
told to 'meditate on the Law day and night'. Mary
'pondered all these things in her heart', and Jesus
clearly meditated on God's word throughout his
life, and drew the appropriate truths out of his
storehouse of wisdom as the situation required.

The monastic movement was a renewal movement fired by hunger for God's Word. Particularly
with few written copies of the scriptures available,
writing God's Word 'on the heart' was about the
only place most people could afford to write it.
More recently, the Navigator movement was built
largely upon the foundation of memorising scripture. Jean Darnell, a fine American Pentecostal
pastor who worked in the United Kingdom for
several decades, used to give people whom she
counselled, a 'scripture prescription' which was
to be 'repeated three times daily after meals'!

I think of a young mother who was struggling in
her relationship with her eldest child, and went to
her vicar to ask for help—specifically for a verse.
He gave her Romans 5:5, 'God has poured our his
love into our hearts by the Holy Spirit, whom he
has given us.' This mother did not so much hide it
in her heart, as clung to it desperately as if it were
a rope attached to a life-raft. She can see, looking
back, that it was indeed a life-line. It kept her
afloat, built in her confidence in what God could
do. Notice it is God who *has* already shed abroad

his love, by the Holy Spirit who *has* been given
to us. It was an inspired text to give, because it
did not tell her anything that she ought to do or
be, but simply stated and affirmed what God had
already done.

Entering the story

So far we have thought about a single phrase,
sentence or verse of scripture entering into us
and becoming rooted and growing to shape our
character and actions. This is the picture that
Paul holds out to us in such faith-building words
in 2 Corinthians. He had been speaking about a
veil being over the eyes of the Israelites when
the Old Covenant is read. He then goes on to
say:

> But whenever anyone turns to the Lord, the
> veil is taken away. Now the Lord is the Spirit,
> and where the Spirit of the Lord is, there is
> freedom. And we, who with unveiled faces
> all reflect the Lord's glory, are being trans-
> formed into his likeness with ever-increasing
> glory, which comes from the Lord, who is the
> Spirit. (2 Cor 3:16–18)

However, there is another way in which we can
see and read scripture. Rather than taking a verse
into ourselves, we can step into a whole story. This
is at the heart of Ignatian spirituality. It involves
using the imagination and finding ourselves in the
story.

As we saw back in Chapter Two (An Open Door),
stories are very important to us all in helping us

find our place in life. Jews find their identity as the Exodus community, and Christians are held together—despite many, and often trivial differences—by the Jesus story. Families (and churches) have stories which shape their identity. The two communities in Northern Ireland find their identity in two different stories that go back hundreds of years, as do the warring factions in the former state of Yugoslavia. This is why the problems are so difficult to deal with. It is the stories that must be addressed, not just—or primarily—the points on which there is disagreement.

We know how important stories are for children, and what security and peace they experience when a story is read to them over and over again. It touches their soul, for stories are a powerful means of finding our identity.

There are many different temperaments amongst people, but in many ways we tend to connect with reality most easily either by thinking (having rational thoughts in verbal form), or through our feelings (we see life through the varied hues of our many different emotions), or by action (using the sensors of our five senses to find our way through life), or by intuition (our instincts and our 'feel' for what is possible, right or true). It helps to know how we most easily relate to life. It will affect how we pray. Remember we all function in all these ways, it is just a matter of knowing which is the main road into our inner life. In prayer it is good to start with that approach, and then to seek to develop also the other avenues into 'knowing'.

With that in mind we can read a story and enter it though our imagination, trying to picture the colour of the trees that Jonah sat under, the

scale of the waters that were held back when
the Israelites crossed the Red Sea, the feelings
of the shepherds on the way to Bethlehem, the
arguments Pilate's wife might have used to get
him to hand Jesus over, and so on.

As we do this we will find ourselves addressed
by the story. I led a group once through Joshua's
experience before the battle of Jericho (Jos 5:13–15).
When I asked people afterwards to share what
they had experienced, one person said they found
themselves being asked the question 'What are
the sandals I should be taking off?' Interestingly
they said they did not know what the answer was,
but they knew the question mattered in their relationship with God. This is a reminder of the prayer
principle of sowing and reaping. Knowing and
being known do not always, or normally, yield to
instant answers. Staying with unanswered questions is an important way of listening to God.

There is a prayer exercise at the end of this
chapter which is intended to help in 'entering
the story of scripture'. Melvyn Matthew's book,
The Hidden Word (Darton, Longman and Tod,
London, '92) is a helpful aid to this way of relating
to scripture.

One way in which this whole aspect of knowing
God was opened up for me happened when I
decided to read the parable of the Prodigal Son as
my only reading of scripture for a month. Initially
it was, quite frankly, boring. I knew it so well, I
could hardly keep my eyes on the page and read
the words. But after about the fourth day I saw
something I had not seen before. That happened
again the next day, and most days. I ended the
month 'entering into the story of the Prodigal Son'
with a sense of enthusiasm and anticipation.

Conclusion

We have considered two ways in which we can
harness scripture to our prayer life. One is by
planting seeds of God's Word into our hearts. They
will be 'bite-sized' portions that we can digest and
'chew over'. The other is by immersing ourselves
in the stories of scripture and finding ourselves
in them. There are two exercises below which are
expressions of these two ways of entering scripture
and allowing it to enter us. Once you have become
familiar with these specific exercises, they should
enable you to use almost any text, and any story
in scripture, through which to strengthen prayer
as a means of encountering God.

PRAYER EXERCISE 1: Receiving the seed of God's Word

Chose a verse of scripture which you want to see
planted and bearing fruit in your life.

Here are three contrasting possibilities, but
much of scripture can be handled in this way.

For seeing the presence of God and the presence
of the holy in the whole of life
*'Take off your sandals, for the place where you are
standing is holy ground.'*

To grasp the wonder of the humanity of Christ as
seen in his befriending of Zacchaeus
*'Come down immediately. I must stay at your
house today.'*

To be shaped and filled by the love revealed to us
in the actions, character and heart of God.

'God has poured out his love into our hearts by the Holy Spirit, whom he has given us.'

Sit down and relax.
With hands open upwards in an attitude of faith and receiving, focus first on God, his presence with you and his love towards you.

Then recite the verse slowly several times (half a dozen or more).
Repeat the scripture slowly.
Say it with faith, receiving it into your being.
Make the pauses longer between each repetition.
If a response comes to mind, speak it out.
– it may be a simple 'thank you, Jesus' or something longer
– do not ramble on: a sentence or two is enough.
The moment you feel as if you are 'drying up', repeat the verse.

It is good to decide beforehand how long you are going to do this for—say 5 or 10 minutes.—then keep to that, and do it regularly: using the same verse for several weeks at a time.

The important principle is not to strive. If you have no spontaneous response, flow back into repeating the scripture. If you spend ten minutes slowly repeating and receiving the scripture, you will have ministered the truth into your inner being. If you have a response express it, if you do not, return into repeating the scripture.

In this way you take the truth into yourself, you plant the seed of the Word in your life. You plant the acorn. God promises that 'they will be called oaks of righteousness, a planting of the Lord, for the display of his splendour.' (Is 61:3)

PRAYER EXERCISE 2: Entering the story of scripture

To aid this exercise the story is printed here. It is from Mark 10:46–52.

> Then they came to Jericho. As Jesus and his disciples, together with a large crowd, were leaving the city, a blind man, Bartimaeus (that is, the Son of Timaeus), was sitting by the roadside begging. When he heard that it was Jesus of Nazareth, he began to shout, 'Jesus, Son of David, have mercy on me!'
> Many rebuked him and told him to be quiet, but he shouted all the more, 'Son of David, have mercy on me!'
> Jesus stopped and said, 'Call him.'
> So they called to the blind man, 'Cheer up! On your feet! He's calling you.'
> Throwing his cloak aside, he jumped to his feet and came to Jesus.
> 'What do you want me to do for you?' Jesus asked him.
> The blind man said, 'Rabbi, I want to see.'
> 'Go,' said Jesus, 'your faith has healed you.'
> Immediately he received his sight and followed Jesus along the road.

Enter this story in your imagination.
Mingle with the crowd, sense the heat of the day, the swirling dust, the growing tiredness, and maybe irritability of those following Jesus that day.
Be one of the first to catch sight of Bartimaeus, notice your reactions.

Watch the disciples (like bouncers) trying to keep
some order in the place.
- imagine what they might be saying to each other
  or to Bartimaeus.
- notice your feelings as the story develops.

Take time to see yourself as a disciple.
- let their understandable, but un-kingdom like
  response challenge your excuses about it being
  'not appropriate' to live by the values of the age
  to come.

Feel the whole story from Bartimaeus's perspective
- the long years of despair and frustration
- the quickening spark of hope based on stories
  he would have heard
- the courage and desperation behind his full-
  throated shout for help
- his total disinterest in respectability and social
  propriety—if he could be healed . . .
Let yourself be Bartimaeus, cry out to God for the
healing you need.

Watch Jesus
- with time, awareness, compassion, authority.

Respond to the whole event with
- *praise* to Jesus for who he is and what he
  does, and
- with *trusting* openness, like Bartimaeus, to
  his power to break into the difficult parts of
  your life.

Chapter 8

Listening Prayer
Encountering God Within

*Our specifically human existence consists
precisely in our hearing the Word of God.
We are what we hear from God.*
Emil Brunner, *The Divine Imperative* p.66

*Who can ever master something in which
the main object is to be mastered?*
Richard Foster, *Prayer* (Hodder & Stoughton,
London. '92) p.xi

It has not been easy to resist the urge, at the
start of each chapter, to say 'this is the heart
of prayer', or 'this is the most important part of
this book'. I will continue to resist that temptation
because there are other equally important aspects
of prayer to come. However, it can certainly be
said that this is the least practised or appreciated
dimension of prayer. 'Prayer' for most people, and
probably for most Christians, is about talking *to*
God, *telling* him about our needs, and—if we
could but see it—*giving* him the benefit of our
wisdom and advice. In church situations, where
people come forward at the end of a service or
meeting to be prayed for, I have found time and

time again that so many are as eager to tell God their needs as they are deaf to any idea that they might get an answer. As someone has poured out their heart to God, with me alongside them, they have finished what they have to say, and got up to walk away. I have often had to say 'How about waiting for an answer?' The truth is that the more important part of prayer is what God says to us, how he shapes and directs us.

The previous three chapters in particular have prepared us for this stage in prayer. We have already engaged with listening prayer in those chapters, doing some important ground work. We cannot hear God aright unless there is some degree of self-acceptance and affirmation of who I am as a new creation in Christ. Without that first step, there is nowhere for the seed of the word to be planted. Equally, unless we are in touch with the old 'diseased self', and the distortions it brings to our whole way of seeing life, God, and particularly ourselves, we will be poor receivers of what God is saying to us. Moreover, unless our hearing from God is rooted in relationship to him through scripture, we will be at the mercy of every whim or fad or notion—and take them for the voice of God.

So what more is there to listening prayer than has already been considered?

Living in response to God

The first thing to underline is that to be a disciple is to be someone who has chosen to live life in response to what God is saying to us. This is where the idea of life as a journey or pilgrimage is so

helpful. Too often we 'settle down' (as Abraham
and his father had done before God's call came
to Abraham—see Gen 11:31b) and think we have
arrived. You hardly need any instruction if that is
the case. You have life sorted out, there is nothing
to do but 'live happily ever after'. If, however, you
see life as a journey then you will continually need
to consult the map, consider which fork in the road
to choose, and consult the best guide available.
Listening prayer has that sense of journey about
it. It is the practice of what king David was
continually reported as doing, namely 'enquiring
of the Lord'.

This is the heart of conversion. It is a turning
around from running and directing my own life,
to living in response to God's call, choosing his
word and his way. Indeed the word 'listen' means
'to obey', because it has about it that quality of
listening that takes what is said 'to heart', and
acts upon it.

Jesus our model

We see in the life of Jesus a wonderful example
of what it means to live by listening, to live in
response to God's call upon our lives. It is evident
in two particular ways; how he began his ministry
and how he continued it.

The ministry of Jesus began in his baptism, in
the course of which he heard the Father addressing him in the words: 'You are my Son, whom I
love; with you I am well pleased' (Lk 3:22). Notice
that he heard the Father address him through
the words of scripture. This is why learning to
pray back the scriptures is so vital to the work of

listening prayer. It is often in the act of praying
them back, that they reach down and take hold of
us, becoming God's living word to us.

Notice also that the word came to Jesus on
two levels. First, there was powerful personal
affirmation. To be assured of relationship to God,
and security in his totally accepting love, is good
news indeed. The great 'I am's' of John's gospel
grew in the fertile soil of such acceptance by his
heavenly Father. So many of the voices we hear,
and allow into our hearts to shape our actions, are
destructive of that foundation of self-worth before
God. As John Bradshaw puts it:

> Jesus said: 'Before Abraham was, I am.'
> They crucified him for this.
> The old order crucifies all of us
> for expressing our I amness and creativity.
> (John Bradshaw *Homecoming* [Piatkus,
>   London: '90] p.274)

We must train our hearts to listen to the affirming
word. It is foundational to our very being. We are
'becoming people', people in a lifelong process of
becoming who we are. That becoming happens in
response to others. We are 'called into being'. We
do not find it within, but by being addressed by one
who loves, accepts, affirms, and mirrors back to us
our true self. This is what God does in prayer—if
we will dare to listen. First, then we can expect to
hear words of personal affirmation.

But there was another side to the voice that
spoke to Jesus. The affirming word strengthened
his sense of being; yet hidden within that word
was a call into mission. The 'word from the

Father' was an amalgam of two Old Testament scriptures; one about David's royal reign (Ps 2:7), and the other taken from the song of the Suffering Servant (Is 42:1). No one before had put together kingship and suffering. That word became the agenda for the whole life and mission of Jesus—to bring in the kingdom of God by way of suffering love. Notice here, as we saw in Chapter Two, that this encounter with God was not just for that particular moment, but for the whole of his life. How important it is for us to listen and draw strength and direction from our encounters with God.

We too then, are to expect God to both affirm our sense of worth before him, and give us directions for ordering our lives around the coming of his kingdom and the doing of his will.

Jesus, the one who listened

Though Jesus is spoken of in scripture as the Word of God and the Word-made-flesh, it is also true that in revealing true humanity to us, he has shown that it consists of a continual process of listening to God. To be human is be a Word-receiving being. A vital part of that process is an eagerness and determination to listen. The following scriptures show how this theme of life as a response to the Word which God addresses to us, was central to who Jesus was, as well as to what he did:

'Man does not live on bread alone, but on every word that comes from the mouth of God.' (Matt 4:4)

'My mother and brothers are those who hear
God's word and put it into practice.' (Lk
8:21)

'My food,' said Jesus, 'is to do the will of
him who sent me and to finish his work.'
(Jn 4:34)

'I tell you the truth, the Son can do nothing
by himself; he can do only what he sees his
Father doing, because whatever the Father
does the Son also does.' (Jn 5:19)

All that Jesus says about 'his hour' is part of this
process of not taking the law, or life, into his own
hands, but listening to the leading and directing
of the Father.

In summary, in the life of Jesus we see that
his primary encounter with the Father addressed
both his being and his doing, and that this became
foundational to his whole living. He first listened
to the word the Father was addressing to him, and
then acted accordingly. If this was true of Jesus
then it must be vital for us as his followers, to be
in the company of those who listen to God. How
is it to be done? I want to answer that question by
speaking first from personal experience, and then
spelling out some basic principles.

Part of my journey

Over the last two years I have moved from sensing
God putting the thought of a move into my mind,
to having that confirmed, finding the right move,
and beginning to settle into a new work. As I look

back I can see that God has spoken in a number of ways.

It probably began in the *emotions* as a certain loss of motivation. There were difficult tasks and great challenges in the life of the church, and nothing seemed straightforward, nor did my insights immediately win the day or the argument. That was no different from the previous twenty years in the same job. What was different was a lack of energy to find a way through. So my listening began by listening to my feelings—before God. Did I need a break, was I working too hard, had I lost my first love? These questions naturally come to the fore, though I had already discovered that just because an idea is based on a critical view of oneself, does not mean that it is what God is saying. Nor is the opposite true.

What happened cut right across all that thinking with a '*word from God*' that was very specific: 'This work has been a fruitful field, but now the time has come to plough it up for the next harvest, and you are to have no part in that.' It is difficult to get clearer marching orders! How did that word come? I can only say that 'one day it was there'. (I have often found that a word from God is suddenly there.) I never saw it coming. Keeping a journal was almost certainly crucial to my catching the word when it came, since my experience is that God's word comes more like a butterfly on the shoulder than a thunderbolt on the head.

There followed a long period (at least, it felt like that at the time!) of *silence*. I was seeking a move, with little or nothing coming. One or two possibilities appeared on the horizon. With some of them I convinced myself that this was 'it', only to see them disappear back over the horizon. This

created a wilderness sensation, a lack of hearing
from God—or anyone. But God speaks in and
through the silence. He makes himself known
by his absence. That divine withdrawal led to
a vital time of personal growth in which I had
to address feelings of self-pity (disguised pride),
and come to a fuller sense of acceptance before
God for who I am, rather than what I do. Dark
and difficult though it was it was a time of giving
and blessing.

I was sustained in that by two verses which
leapt out of the pages of *scripture* at me. The
first, was 'the Lord delights in those who fear
him, who put their hope in his unfailing love'
(Ps 147:11). It was followed a few weeks later by
my sensing the description of Abraham as God's
call on my life. The writer to the Hebrews says he
'went, even though he did not know where he was
going' (Heb 11:8). As I continued to listen before
God I became aware that he was separating me
from my identity as a clergyman—to be a person,
not just a parson.

Two further elements contributed to the comple-
tion of this process. First, the prayer of friends, who
had some *pictures* that related to how my present
job appeared. It kept on coming back—despite some
serious evasive action on my part. The picture was of
a film being developed. Evidently it involves dipping
the film in the solution again and again, until the
picture is clear. That was what was happening with
this particular possibility.

The final stage was a sense of *call from the
church*. I had often said that while the church
today tests the 'call' of those putting themselves
forward for ordination, the New Testament suggests a pattern of the church working the other

way round. The church then seems rather to
have done the calling into ministry. Now I was
experiencing it first hand, for it was what leaders
in the church were saying to me about my suitabil-
ity for the work, not what I felt, that constituted
the call.

Drawing some lessons

I have told this story in some detail as often stories tell more than bare principles. My experience
underlined to me that listening is a way of life,
and that God speaks in 'many and varied' ways;
through scripture, by a direct word from him,
through others, in experience, through dreams,
and through silence. All have a part to play.
Keeping a journal has proved crucial to listening;
otherwise what is being said disappears like a
morning mist.

However, this is a story of listening at the easier
end of the spectrum of life, namely about an outward issue of a job and a move. The other end of the
spectrum—listening to God about my own journey
into growth as a person—is more important and
more elusive; though the two are bound together.
It is this moving forward in personal growth that
is vital to life and to true discipleship.

It is about this aspect of listening that I want to
identify some ways that are important. But first
let me answer the question that is sometimes
raised at this point; namely, 'How do you set
about listening?' The basic answer is to make
time to be quiet and unhurried. Simply being
still with nothing else to hand, and no deadline
to meet, is what is needed to listen. The question

is, do I make time for such prayer, or is my prayer
all busy and 'getting on' prayers?

PRAYER OF THE HEART:
Calming our hearts to listen

Calm me O Lord as you stilled the storm
Still me O Lord, keep me from harm
Let all the tumult within me cease
Enfold me Lord in your peace
(from David Adam, *The Edge of Glory*
[Triangle, London. '85] p.8)

Although I have sometimes spent a whole day
at a time, my more usual listening prayer is done
over a half to three-quarters of an hour period.
The most difficult part is simply to make the
time and to give it priority. The next step, and
next most difficult part, is to still my heart, and
turn my thoughts to God. The exercise at the end
of Chapter One on 'letting go' is a great help in
slowing the pace down and enabling me to be on
God's wavelength; indeed, I find it helpful to see
myself as a radio receiver being tuned in to the
eternal frequency of truth and love. The listening
then often has three stages within in. They are not
neat and tidy compartments and I do not always
major on all three, but they are three elements
that are important in listening.

Stage one: Listen to life

This is the obvious starting point; to reflect on,
and listen to, what life has been saying to us—or
rather what God has been saying to us through
life. Included in this are several elements.

Listening to our experience of life. Reviewing
what has been happening to us, and the events
which define our life at present, is an obvious
place to begin. The important thing is to seek to
discern what God is saying to us through those
experiences; as Neville Ward has put it:

> every experience is a kind of annunciation.
> (J. Neville Word, *Five for Sorrow, Ten for Joy*
> [Darton, Longman and Todd, London; '93] p. 3)

The natural instinct is to review our experience
with a view to blaming others and proving ourselves right. Before Love, which accepts us fully,
we can however dare to listen to the fuller picture.
In particular we are to seek to discern what God
is saying to us. Sometimes he is calling us to trust
him with the unknown, and at other times he is
calling us to rise up and resist the evil or injustice
that confronts us or others. Not infrequently I
have felt a sense of 'here we go again', as a
repeated pattern emerges. It is important to listen
to such patterns because they often tell us what we
are reluctant to face and find a way through. Having considered what is happening, it is important
to go on to ask why this is happening to me, and
more importantly still, what is God saying through
this experience?

Listening to our motivation. Often God is wanting us to see the true motivation for our actions.
He does this, not in order to blame us, but rather to
set us free from being 'driven', rather than 'called'
people. Am I continually overworking, getting into
debt, losing my temper, being put down at work,
or whatever? When we have identified a repeated
pattern, we can then bring it to God in prayer

and seek the gift of interpretation. It does not always come immediately, not because God has a problem thinking up an answer, but because we have a problem hearing answers.

Listening to our emotions. All too easily we project unacknowledged feelings onto other people. Before God we can dare to own those feelings and discern what we are to do about them. Only when we are honest about them, can we handle them well and have some confidence that they are informing rather than distorting our judgement. The process involves getting in touch with what we feel, and then naming it. Just like Adam naming the animals, and thereby giving them their identity, we need to do the same with our feelings.

We then apply our minds to consider why we are feeling this way, and can then go on—before God—to choose the right response. It may be to 'have it out with someone', or to forgive another person, to choose to do something, or to await God's timing. It is that choosing of the response before God that enables us to hear. Remember we are called upon to overcome evil with good. Listening to our emotions enables us to shift into a more creative gear than retaliation. It equips us to respond to life, rather than react to it.

Stage two: Listening to desires

Stage one is about listening in a re-active, albeit creative, way to what is happening to us. This next stage involves our participating with God in shaping life. Jesus said that he came to give us life 'in all its abundance'. There are hopes, desires and hidden energies and vitality in all of us. Listening prayer is a way of mining those resources.

We are often inhibited in this work because of a low self-image, and because we feel that somehow the Christian should have no will of their own. The opposite is the truth. God wants us to be fully human, fully alive. That means having a strong and healthy will—harnessed to God's will ('your kingdom come, your will be done'). Here are two people who have much to teach us in this matter of getting in touch with these deepest desires within us.

> Desire, in my opinion, is among the most important of these radiant things that must be allowed to surface . . . It takes the real self to truly desire, and in its desiring all that is good, beautiful, and true, it more quickly and wonderfully functions in the image of its Maker.
> (Leanne Payne, *The Broken Image* [Kingsway Publications, Eastbourne. '81] p.151/2)

> If we were able to discover what we really want, if we could become conscious of the deepest desire within us, then we should have discovered God's will . . . The saint is the person who has discovered his/her deepest desire. They then 'do their own thing', which is also God's thing.
> (Gerard Hughes, *God of Surprises* [Darton, Longman and Todd, London. '85] p.62)

To be in touch with desire is to be in touch with life from Above—within. It is no easy task, for they are easily buried by the pressures of living, the fear

of failure, and the loss of the true self. In seeking
to re-connect with them we may well discover
how the true self has been put to death, and
needs awakening. But in this pursuit, life breaks
forth; resurrection, new creation. In a culture that
has harnessed desire to false gods and unhealed
emotions, and now lacks joy, and hope, desire is
also needed for our survival as a people. Truly, as
James Houston puts it: 'The absence of desire can
kill prayer' (*Prayer, the transforming friendship*
[Lion, Oxford. '89] p.48.)

Stage three: Listening for the divine word

In listening to life, and to desire, we listen to
God. Yet there is a specific, focused listening to
God which is also to take place. We are to wait
before God for him to address us. It may well be
a word that comes through and in our listening
to life and to desire. But there is also simply a
holding of ourselves before God for him to speak
truth, life, and light into our souls.

Often this comes, particularly initially, in seemingly 'banal' form which we hesitate to share with
others. We are not to despise the day of small
things if they speak to us and touch our heart.
'I love you', 'You are special to me', are not to
be dismissed, but received, and cherished. Out of
them will grow richer, stronger words that renew
our inner life, sharpen our hearing. In this address
by God we also encounter the 'easy yoke' of which
Jesus spoke, the being joined to him, which sets
us free from diseased attitudes within and false
pressures without. It is indeed the life-giving word

that nourishes the soul. It comes to those who hold themselves before God with openness to all that he desires to give them.

PRAYER EXERCISE: Listening

With paper, or prayer journal, and pen at the ready, set aside ten, twenty or thirty minutes to listen to God. It is best to start with just ten minutes, and build from there. Do not be discouraged if you feel you hear nothing to begin with. Remember, although you cannot recall how many steps you took before you learned to walk, you know it was a skill worth developing even if it took a thousand failures.

Prepare yourself with two minutes of 'letting go and receiving from God'.

You may well find that there are, in practice, three distinct exercises in this one exercise. Simply get as far as you can in your agreed time. Not having enough time is a good thing; it spurs us on to come back and listen again.

Listening to life

Reflect on your recent experience of life.
– what are the major events?
– what have been the dominant emotions?
– what is life 'calling out of you'?
– what response do you sense God calling you to make.

Listening to desires

You may have to go back many years to get in touch with hopes and dreams and desires.

From the last such time you can recall, work
forward, and recall any moments
– of longing, elation, joy, hope, harmony.
See them as God's gifts to you on your journey
of faith.
– ask him to show you how to hold onto those
  moments and draw strength from them.
Ask for insight to see how they, rather than events
  around you, should shape your life and your
  priorities.

Listening to God

Give thanks to God for his life in you and his love
for you.
Be still, turn your head, and hands and thoughts
up to God in openness.
– simply ask him to speak to you.
– write down what comes to you.
Do not try to hear so much as focus on him—the
word comes most easily in the embrace of the
Beloved.
Receive every gift with thanksgiving, noting it
down, and pondering it in your heart.

PART FOUR

GOING

Chapter 9

Intercession
Encountering God in Prayer for Others

Prayer is a way of life which begins and ends in love.
Roberta Bondi, *To Pray and to Love*, p. 8

We are called to be physicians of that civilisation about which we dream, the civilisation of love.
Pope Paul VI, Dec 31st 1975

The third stage in the journey of prayer, after we have entered into *seeing* the wonder of God, and following on from our being in the process of *knowing* God and being changed into his likeness, is our *going* out 'to live and work to your praise and glory', as the Anglican liturgy puts it.

This going has two distinct stages. First we 'go' in prayer, and then we are to go in action, though—as we shall see in the chapter 'Practising the Presence of God'—we never go from God's presence. Rather, that second stage of going, is a going with and into his presence: 'Surely I am with you always, to the very end of the age' (Matt 28:20). In the next two chapters we will consider

how we are to 'go' in prayer: that is, how we are
to turn our thoughts out to the world around us
and, in intercession, give attention to the needs
of the world. In doing so, we fulfil the second
great commandment, to love others. The final
two chapters will then consider how we go in
action and retain awareness of the reality of God's
presence and action in our lives.

There is a real danger, particularly in the me-
centred culture in which we live, that we never
do break out from self-concern in prayer. It is
this that makes intercession seem like hard work.
It is also one reason why we need to pray for
the world—so that we might be liberated from
self-concern. Richard Lovelace writes about those
who are:

> so tied up in programs of spiritual self-
> improvement that they have no time to care
> about anything but the throbbing self-concern
> at the centre of their consciousness . . .

he reminds us rather that:

> radical faith in Christ frees the Christian
> from spiritual self-concern to give attention
> to God and others, and to think and pray
> about the reformation of structures.
> (Richard Lovelace, *Dynamics of Spiritual Life*,
>   [Paternoster Press, Exeter. '79] p.383/4)

Having explored earlier how to use scripture as
a resource for prayer, I want now to continue
that theme, by looking at intercession from the
starting point of praying back the prayers of

scripture. What I am proposing is that we see the prayers in scripture as the fertile soil out of which intercession can grow. Once we have such soil we can then plant out our own particular flowers of prayer for the needs of others.

The art of sensible praying

I do not mean to use the word sensible in the way we immediately think of it; namely the parental admonition to be sensible and not cause anyone any trouble. I use it rather in the more creative and enriching sense of praying with our senses, not least in touch with our emotions. Prayer is to be whole-hearted, that is, done with the whole heart. And with the body too.

We have so much to learn from Jewish traditions of prayer. Their most famous place of prayer is the Wailing Wall: it must be difficult to pray there if your prayer is all in the mind, and you are not in touch with your feelings. For emotions are a vast resource for prayer; they can energise prayers of grief, compassion, anger and justice. As we pray for the world it will greatly enrich our praying if we make contact with our emotions and pray with passion (literally: strong feelings).

PRAYER PRINCIPLE SIX
THE PRAYER OF ATTITUDE
Prayer is not just a matter of words, it engages with every part of us. We need to develop the use of our emotions, imagination, intuition and senses. We can then learn to prayer though our attitude, even without formulating words.

Our bodies are also a great prayer resource.
Again, the normal Jewish physical posture is
most instructive. It is one of standing, with head
raised looking up to heaven and hands open wide,
expressive of openness and vulnerability. It is a
posture which expresses full confidence in how we
will be received by the One to whom we make
ourselves vulnerable.

In contrast, the normal Western Christian posture for prayer is seated, head bowed (in shame?),
eyes closed (in case we see the world?) and head
clasped in the hands (lest we hear anything?). As
a grief posture it is quite appropriate; but there is
more to prayer than grief. What is more, I suspect
that the grief being expressed is about ourselves
('I am a worm and not a man' Ps 22:6!), and lack of
self-acceptance, rather than any sense of entering
into the pain and anguish of the world.

In this connection I notice an interesting contrast between what Jesus did and what he taught.
He taught us, in prayer, to 'go into your room,
close the door and pray' (Matt 6:6); whereas what
he did was to go into the desert and hills. There is
a place for both, and some may not have access to
their own space (though that may be rare today),
whilst others do not have ready access to the
countryside. However, even in a town, we can walk
and pray. I find that walking keeps my body active
(it is difficult to fidget *and* walk, for walking is a
way of planned fidgeting). Walking frees my mind
and spirit to pray. Especially if anger is fuelling
my prayer, walking energetically is a good way of
expressing it.

We can also use our other senses, such as sight,
to add vitality to our praying. If our concern,
for example, is for Northern Ireland, we can get

a picture that expresses the struggles of that
community. A picture of one of the IRA or UVF
end-of-terrace murals can put us in touch with
the deep fear, hatred and prejudice that covers
the land. Or a picture of Gordon Wilson, who so
courageously bore witness to his faith by forgiving
those who killed his daughter, can aid our praying
for the raising up of a generation of Christians who
will endeavour, despite the cost, to overcome evil
with good. (See further on this in the section on
making a prayer journal, in the Postscript.)

The rosary is a means of prayer that is connected to the sense of touch. Neville Ward's book,
Five for Sorrow, Ten for Joy, is a fine Methodist
meditation and instruction on its use. It is worth
remembering that Wesley's rosary is one of the
'holy relics' still kept today. Those of us with a
Protestant background may shy away from such
an aid to prayer. We may have to get in touch with
prejudice to break free. Equally we may need to
find other 'touching aids to prayer'. I have a tree
stump from a peat bog in Scotland in my prayer
'line of sight'. Though I do not touch it much,
I often look at it and reflect on the beauty of
that piece of wood shaped under great pressure
for two hundred years. It is an aid to praying
for creation and for society for it was laid down
through that horrific act of vandalism towards
creation and injustice towards the needy, by the
Clearances that so scarred the countryside and the
community in Scotland in the past. It inspires me
to pray against similar injustices today, as well as
to have confidence that God cares for the abused
and can sculpture beauty even out of injustice.
In these, and other ways, we are to stretch our
praying skills and use our whole being in prayer.

With this preliminary, we turn now to the prayers
of scripture. In doing so I want to draw attention to
four great themes of those prayers. As you explore
and practise these themes other ones may well
come to you. In that case, integrate them into
your prayer for the world.

Hope

I could, equally well, have used the words 'despair'
or 'lament', for what seems to give energy and
urgency to so many of the prayers of scripture
is the gulf between what is and what could or
ought to be. It is this gap which provokes and
kindles prayer. Just as an electric current will
jump between two points, creating a spark which
can ignite a fire, a cooker or an engine, so prayer
which sees the gap between what is and what
should be, can ignite a major work of God. Which
is why lament, grief, and wailing play such a part
in biblical prayers.

Hannah weeps before the Lord for a child, and is
neither put off by Eli accusing her of being drunk,
nor by her husband saying 'Don't I mean more to
you than ten sons?' (1 Sam 1:8). Hannah's state
is as clear an answer as he could wish to have, if
only he could see it! Hezekiah's prayer for healing,
and Bartimaeus' prayer for sight, both express the
same agonised struggle to discover from God what
seems a million miles from where they are.

At a national level, Nehemiah (Neh 1) grieves
over the state of Jerusalem, not just because of
the bad state it is in, but because it is so far from
God's purpose for his city. Moses on the mountain

cries out for Israel because they are so wayward,
so far from God's plan for them. Daniel's prayer
for Jerusalem (Dan 9:4–19, especially 17–19), or
Paul's prayer for Israel (Rom. 9–11, and especially
9:1–4, and 10:1) follow this same 'gulf dynamic' of
grief and hope.

So I could have headed this section 'grief' or
'lament', but I have entitled it hope (the other
end of the spectrum) because we live in a society
so lacking in hope. It may be easier for us to
be in touch with what is wrong than with what
the coming of the kingdom might look like. This
is so because in the West, this century which
began with high (humanistic) hopes of progress,
is ending on a note of hopelessness. Apart from a
hope that things may get better materially, there
is little or no other hope. As Mother Teresa so
rightly said, in the West at present there is 'a
famine of hope'. Much of the urban violence and
pointless vandalism is an outworking at the social
level of hopelessness. As is the use of drugs. So, for
example, one of my prayers recently was simply a
response to a throwaway line in a TV news item,
that there are 10,000 drug addicts in Glasgow. My
response was to pray for hope, meaning, purpose,
value and self worth to be poured out on that
drug community—through the church in that
fine city.

Which is just why Christian prayer should focus
on hope, and draw on the riches of scripture to that
end. Not that hope should be used as a sticking
plaster to remove the ugly sight of despair, but as
the salve to wash people's wounds.

The kingdom is the primary picture when it
comes to praying down hope: 'Your kingdom come'
is the fundamental Christian prayer. Our prayers

will be greatly enriched if we take hold of the
promises of God and pray that they may come
to fulfilment in the life of the world and be
embodied in the life of the church. We can use
Ephesians 5:22–32 to pray for marriages, and
for the church as the Bride of Christ. Ephesians
3:14–21 is a wonderful prayer to 'pray back' (in
the manner outlined in Chapter Seven) on behalf
of individuals or church communities, not least
those going through times of testing or upheaval,
that they may embody what Pope Paul VI called
a civilisation of love.

Some of the servant songs of Isaiah can give life
to our prayers for the life of the nation and the
world community. I have found the flow of Isaiah
chapter 11 another helpful pattern to rest on in
my praying for communities and nations. The
flow is from weakness (11:1), through likeness
(11:2–3) to justice (11:3–5) and on into peace for
the whole created order (11:6–9) and God's purposes through his people (11:10–16). It formed a
fruitful basis of prayer amongst a group of church
leaders recently, together with a written prophecy
about what God was doing in the world. Together
these two resources enlarged our vision, and so
strengthened and guided our praying. We are to
harness our prayers to the hope that is revealed
in scripture.

Character

If we could stand back from our prayers for others,
just for a moment, we would see how easily we
pray for improved circumstances but how difficult

we find it to pray for enlarged character. Yet the
emphasis in scripture is much more on character
than circumstances.

When we pray for healing, when we 'share our
prayer needs', and when we pray for one another
in difficulties, we focus on praying for life to be
easier. Now, I do not want to discourage prayer
for healing, or loving concern for people going
through difficult times such as marriage breakdown, bereavement, or redundancy. What I must
do, however, because the scriptures tell us so, is to
point out that most prayers in scripture are about
people remaining faithful under pressure rather
than about the end of the pressure.

Typical of such an approach are Paul's prayer
requests from prison. Over half a dozen times he
asks for prayer. Once he asks that he may get out,
but all the rest are prayers that he may 'boldly
declare the gospel' where he is.

The same emphasis on prayer for character above
circumstances is evident in the first recorded prayer
meeting of the early church. Peter and John
had just been released from prison, with strict
instructions 'not to speak or teach at all in the
name of Jesus' (Acts 4:18). They come home to the
believing community who lift up their voice and
spread before God the dire straits that they are
in, ending with the plea 'Now Lord, consider their
threats . . .' (Acts 4:29). Can you imagine how a
Western church might complete that sentence? If
we are honest we would have to admit it would be
about putting an end to this opposition, or about
protecting us from further trouble. But that is not
the prayer of the early church. Theirs is a prayer
for courage to defy orders, the strength to stay true
under duress. So the prayer is:

Now, Lord, consider their threats and . . .
enable your servants to speak your word with
great boldness.

(Acts 4:29)

We normally pray for the circumstances to change,
rather than for the testing and purifying of the
character of the person involved. Frankly it is
embarrassing to do so. And we had better be
careful in moving into this sort of praying. We
are so unused to it that we may all too easily
lapse into judgemental prayers. It is as important
to proceed with caution, as it is to proceed.

If we are to pray in this biblical way, we need
some understanding of why adverse circumstances
befall believers. There seem to be two particular
reasons. First, there is a work of refining and
purifying going on. Peter says:

Now for a little while you may have had
to suffer grief in all kinds of trials. These
have come so that your faith—of greater
worth than gold, which perishes even though
refined by fire—may be proved genuine and
may result in praise, glory and honour when
Jesus Christ is revealed. (1 Pet 1:6–7)

It is important to remember the difference between
testing in an exam, which is to find out whether
you have passed or failed, and the testing by fire
of a metal. The latter testing is always positive. It
will burn out the 'failure' and leave the metal (and,
by analogy, the person) a richer, more valuable
item at the end. Purifying by fire always leaves
metal, and people, finer.

The other reason for difficult experiences in life, is that it is part of our calling to enter into the mission of Christ. It is the result of being holy in a fallen world. We are called to overcome evil with good, and that will take us by way of the Cross. Which is why, although it may be natural to pray for a change of circumstances ('May this cup be taken from me' Matt: 26:39), God may well have some deeper purpose in taking us/others by another way ('Yet not as I will, but as you will' Matt: 26:39). So, for example, it may only be by staying true in the face of false accusations in the work situation, that evil motivation in the person in authority will be creatively confronted. It may seem more 'Christian' to give in, or look the other way, but often confrontation is the calling. Our prayer must be that those so called will be given grace and boldness to overcome evil with good (Rom 12:21). On several occasions I have watched Christians standing up where no one else had the courage to do so. They did it out of a sense of call, as well as a sense of the injustice of the situation. Because they had the support of a loving and praying community, and because they dared (as children of the Father who cares) to risk reputation, employment and prospects in the name of justice, they were able to overcome evil. Our prayer for them is a vital part of the spiritual battle.

It is instructive to use Paul's prayers for the churches to which he wrote. They are full of prayers for character, rather than circumstances. I have found that using them has been a great help. It gives me a starting point, and great riches to ask for. It certainly changes the agenda, which is why we need to let the scriptures be part of

the Spirit's way of lifting us out of an undue
focus in prayer on circumstances, into the gospel
dimension of character.

Compassion

Some of the most moving prayers in scripture are
inspired and fired by compassion; the longing for
the good and welfare of another.

Abraham bargaining with God about how many
righteous people there need to be in Sodom and
Gomorrah before God will spare those cities, is
one such prayer. Moses pleading for his name to
be blotted out if that will enable God to forgive
the children of Israel, is another. Paul's similar
prayer in Romans, noted above, is a parallel New
Testament prayer. Jesus weeping for Jerusalem is
a further example of prayer fuelled by compassion
—as is the whole book of Lamentations in the old
Testament.

One of the values of using these prayers is that
they can often be the means by which God gives
us a like compassion in our prayer for others. For
instance, to pray for our city using the words of
Jesus' prayer for Jerusalem can help us to be in
touch with God's compassion for whole communities—as can the use of the relevant parts of the
book of Jonah. Daniel 9:17–19 is a prayer I have
written out, and frequently use in prayer for our
nation and civilisation.

Furthermore, we know that when we face situations of need and use particular passages of scripture as the basis for our praying, that we are
praying in line with the will of God. We are
entering into his purposes in the world, and we can

have confidence that we are, therefore, praying in line with his will. Without this anchor to our souls, there is always the danger that we will end up simply telling God what to do. As a speaker at General Synod a few years ago graphically put it: 'Most people want to serve God—but only in an advisory capacity!' Praying back the scriptures can deliver us from that approach in prayer.

Blessing

The fourth element of scriptural praying is one of blessing. It was a major feature of the story of the patriarchs in Genesis where charismatic gifting was obviously expected and received as fathers prayed for the next generation. So too we can expect the Spirit to be particularly eager to inspire our praying for the next generation (in family, church, or nation). We can do just that as we use the various blessings of scripture.

We need not restrict ourselves to the parts of scripture that deal with prayer as such, rather we can pray back teaching passages as prayers for others. For example, the description of the sevenfold gifts of the Spirit in Isaiah (IS 11:2–3), or the fruit of the Spirit as defined in Galatians (Gal 5:22–26), or the Beatitudes (Matt 5:3–10), are wonderful material to give strength and direction to our praying for leaders, or others for whom we have a particular responsibility in prayer.

The greatest and most accessible of all such passages, in my experience, is the Aaronic blessing that God told the leaders of Israel to use in putting his name on the people (Num 6:22–27). Putting God's name on someone means stamping them

with the likeness of God, so that they become
an icon of God. That is the basis of the meditative exercise which follows. Remember that such
praying is not to be restricted to praying for those
nearest and dearest to us (though it certainly
does include them). Rather, we are commanded
not only to wish well those we love (which is
what blessing is), but also to pray for those who
misuse us; those who act as if they are enemies
of ours, whether they are conscious of that or not.
We are to bless those who curse and misuse us.
We are to put God's blessing on them. If we are
involved in any form of negative relationship, it
is particularly healthy to take time to use this
meditation as a means of putting God's blessing
on those 'on the other side' of the conflict. By doing
so we are releasing the power of God's kingdom
through our prayers.

   Finally, it is worth pointing out the trinitarian
structure of this blessing. It is the Father who
keeps and protects. It is Jesus who, through his
death, has made grace rather than law, the basis
of our relationship with God and all creation, and
it is the Spirit who brings us peace, shalom, the
wholeness of God mediated to us through his
presence in our lives.

PRAYER EXERCISE: Putting the blessing of God on others.

It is best to learn this blessing by heart, it can then
be part of the way that we bless others throughout the day (see Chapter Twelve, 'Practising the
Presence' for more about blessing). Repeat each
phrase several times 'over the person', either

simply praying wordless prayers of attitude (of blessing) or using the praying back method noted earlier of 'liturgical sentence' (each line of the blessing) with 'charismatic response'. My version is an amalgamation of different translations of this passage.

The Lord bless you and keep you
See the goodness of God streaming out towards the person(s) you are praying for.
God desires their highest good: be open to some insight as to what that might be.
Try to name anything you see (such as courage, joy, forgiveness, energy, love, peace, etc.).

The Psalmist spoke often about God as a Refuge.
- see this person 'entering God's presence' like a strong tower.
- finding there shelter, comfort, and the strength to go on, to keep faith-filled.

The Lord make his face shine upon you and be gracious to you
See Jesus turning to this person, as he did to the woman in the crowd, or to Zacchaeus.
Rejoice in his compassion; see it filling your attitude to the person concerned.
Nathaniel, under the tree, being seen and known by Jesus is another way to see this blessing.
Or Jesus turning and looking on Peter with compassion in the moment of his sin.

To bless is to 'command good': speak out God's goodness, generosity, help, on this person.
- see them being, in C.S. Lewis's words, 'surprised by joy'.

**The Lord lift up the light of his countenance
on you and give you peace**
Know that the Holy Spirit knows this person, or
group, through and through.
There is the smile of God, the waiting of the Father
for the prodigal, upon them.

Name the particular form of God's peace you see
is needed to invade the life of this person.

Peace is a rich Hebrew word that speaks of putting
everything back together
– it is about proper harmony and balance.
– like a bone reset, a relationship healed, a community celebrating the joy of living.
Here is heaven breaking in on earth: see it coming
down and lifting up the person.
See glory from within break out: see the person
experiencing transfiguration by grace.

Chapter 10

Praying the Lord's Prayer

Do not write it on paper;
write in on your heart.
St Augustine, on the Lord's Prayer.

A pattern prayer with few words
but great themes.
Michael Ramsey, *Be Still and Know* (Collins,
Fount Paperbacks, London. '82) p. 27

The Lord's prayer is a summary
of the whole gospel.
Leonardo Boff, *The Lord's Prayer* (the prayer of
integrated liberation) p. 10

The early church did a very thorough job of initiating newcomers into the faith.

That is evidenced both in the New Testament, in which both gospels and epistles are really instruction books to ground new believers in the faith, and also in the work of the church in the first few centuries. That was expressed in the work of the catechumenate, not an easy word to pronounce, or one that we need to repeat often! It refers to the process of preparing candidates for baptism. It was normal for this to take three years

of instruction. Some such schools of Christian
initiation included a major work of preparation
particularly during Lent leading up to baptism
on Easter Eve. It was done then to underline
to the candidates that they were being baptised
into Christ's death and resurrection. What better
day than the one between those two foundational
events of the Christian faith.

The work of nurture of the new believer was
taken very seriously for two particular reasons.

The primary one was that people were coming to faith in a hostile culture, where suffering
was almost inevitable, imprisonment possible, and
martyrdom not out of the question. They had to be
prepared well if they were to cope with whatever
life, the State, and the devil, might throw at them;
especially if martyrdom could be on the list of what
their 'ministry' might be.

The other reason for such thoroughness was
that people were being brought into the faith in
days before the widespread availability of books.
The task of the church was therefore to give people
whatever resources they needed to sustain them
for the whole journey of faith, in a form which
they could remember. Just as today we say to
those new to the faith that reading the Bible and
praying are fundamental to sustain our faith, so
these early Christians were given two particular
resources for Christian living. They were called
the Presentations; not least, because there was
a 'rite of presentation' in which these aids were
given to the candidates.

These two 'Presentations' were like a map and
a compass given to a walker before setting out
on a dangerous journey. They remain part of
the catechumenate of the church today, in places

where that pattern of instruction is consciously
continued, as in the Roman Catholic *Rite of Christian Initiation of Adults* (called simply the RCIA).
Those two Presentations were, and are, as follows:

The Creed

All too easily we see the Creed as a list of doctrines.
It is that, not least as a protection against heresy,
but it is much more than that. As John Sanford
puts it:

> If you listen to the words of the Creed you
> will hear, not a statement of doctrine, but a
> summation of the adventure story of Christ.
> (John Sanford, *The Man who Wrestled with
> God*, p.1)

In other words the Creed is what we might today
call 'a brief history of time' (or 'eternity'?). It is
a distillation of the whole story of God's purposes
in the world, from its original creation, to his revelation in Christ, and on to his ultimate purposes
in the redemption of all creation; complete with
a list of resources to sustain us as we participate
in the great work of creation, namely God's plan
to bring it to fulfilment in Christ. In this short
statement, the new believer was given a summary
of the whole story of scripture. Both the Nicene
Creed, and the later Apostle's, are masterpieces
of writing. They are scripture on the back of
an envelope. Or, rather, in the heart of every
believer.

This meant that when testing times came, the

Christians could remind themselves of God's purposes in the world, and of their calling to be part of that work, even if it included much suffering.

What a rich resource this is for the believer. Indeed, I once heard someone say that 'the two great commandments were spoken by Jesus in 53 words, the Lord's prayer in 63 words, the Apostles Creed in 114 words, the full version of the ten commandments in less than 300 words, but the European Community's regulations on the export of duck eggs runs to 25,000 words!'

The Lord's Prayer

The second of the two great Presentations is the Lord's Prayer. If the Creed reminds us of God's purposes in the whole of creation and the complete course of human history, the Lord's Prayer enables us to find and fulfil our part in that purpose. For to pray 'your kingdom come' is to make ourselves available for God and his purpose in our lives. It is a yielding of ourselves to God through prayer. It is also the means by which we draw on God's wisdom, grace, mercy and strength to fulfil our calling as disciples.

It is, of course, *the* Christian prayer. However, the early Christians had a very different attitude to it than we do today. Apart from anything else it was greatly reverenced. Candidates for baptism were not allowed to know the content of it until well into year two of their initiation, and then they were not allowed to write it down. It was to be written on the heart. This was not only because of the principle we have already considered ('the word spoken is the word believed'),

but because it was considered such a dangerous,
and politically subversive, prayer. That may sur-
prise us because it has become a bland prayer to
many people today. The early church saw it so
differently:

> Allegiance to the empire was determined by
> proclaiming the kingship of the emperors, the
> holiness of their name, and submission to
> their will. To declare otherwise, as demanded
> by praying the Our Father, was to act subver-
> sively towards the powers and principalities.
> (Michael Crosby *Thy Will be Done [Praying
> the Our Father as Subversive Activity]*
> [Orbis Books, Maryknoll. '77] p. 2)

With these two gifts, the Creed and the Lord's
Prayer, the church of the early centuries—a des-
pised, largely uneducated, and persecuted minor-
ity—bore faithful witness to Christ, often to the
point of martyrdom, and eventually conquered
the Roman empire. We do well to sit at their feet
and learn from them how the simple discipline of
this prayer can make us witnesses as fruitful and
faithful to God's grace in our day.

Overfamiliarity, and abuse in its use, have
robbed us of the power and fruitfulness of this
prayer. What follows is an attempt to recapture
it for the life of the church today. To do that there
are four things we need to grasp if we are engage
with its vigour and vitality.

See its shape

We are often not best served by well-intentioned
preachers who, in seeking to teach the Lord's

Prayer, jump straight in to an exposition of it
line by line. Valuable though this is, it misses the
more important fact of the overall shape of the
prayer. Grasping the shape is of more importance
in learning to pray this prayer, than knowing a
great deal about each phrase.

Essentially there is a fourfold pattern.

First is the *address* in which we give attention
to God as he has revealed himself in Christ; the
One who has established intimacy with us as
Father, who has made us a community of faith
which requires us to address him as 'Our' (rather
than 'My') Father, and the One who yet remains,
as Isaiah saw him 'high and lifted up', the One
who inhabits the transcendent glory of heaven.
In other words, the prayer begins with our *seeing*
God, with our beholding the throne. This is always
the first step in prayer, giving attention to the One
to whom we come.

Second, are the *You-prayers*, in which we give
attention to God's name being honoured, his kingdom coming and his will being done. These are
three different ways of saying the same thing,
namely that what God desires and intends is what
matters most to us. Here is the work of conversion
being expressed in our prayers, because our attention is first and foremost on discovering God's will,
and in working on his agenda. We come to God
not to say 'Your will be changed', but 'Your will
be done'.

Third, come the *Us-prayers*, in which we bring
the whole range of our needs to God. Material
needs ('give us'), relational needs ('forgive us'),
and our needs in the face of spiritual conflict
('deliver us'). Yet even these needs are needs
which arise in the course of our seeking to discover

and do God's will and be part of his purposes in the
world. They are the resources we seek to enable
us to go in Christ's name and be involved in the
work of his kingdom. They are the needs we
have if, in the midst of human sin, conflict and
injustice, we are to live and preach the message
of reconciliation. They are the needs of those who
have dedicated their lives to overcoming evil with
good, and—in the process—discover that they are
up against the principalities and powers.

Fourth are the *affirmations* of God's presence
with us: 'the kingdom, the power and the glory
are yours, now and for ever.' Prayer ends by a
faith-affirmation that God is with us as we 'go
out into the world', and that Jesus is with us
'to the very end of the age' as the final words of
Matthew's gospel put it (Matt 28:20).

Notice that the encounter framework of *seeing—knowing—going* lies just below the surface
of this prayer. The address focuses on *seeing* the
One to whom we are coming. The You-prayers
and the Us-prayers are the orientation of our
lives around the will and grace of God. They
express the *knowing* of God which is the fruit
of hungering for his will and his righteousness.
The affirmations speak of the strength in which
we go in his name, they are the practice of God's
presence with us in our *going*.

Once we grasp this overall pattern we can make
best use of the prayer. For example, I was recently
invited by a sick person to pray for them—on
the basis of 'calling for the elders of the church'
(James 5:14). We spent the whole evening praying
the Lord's Prayer. We took a couple of hours to
pray it—though we did have a coffee break in the
middle!

We began by giving attention and worship to
God as the Father in heaven to whom we could
come, with confidence in both his love and his
healing power. This time of worship included
thanksgiving for God's faithfulness to us in the
past, and for his presence with us now. We then
spent time in intercession for ourselves, and particularly the sick person, that God's kingdom
would come, and that we would be able to recognise that coming. Included in this was time
spent in listening payer, being open to what God
might want to say and do through our prayers that
evening.

We then came to the specific needs of the
person who had called us to prayer. In praying for 'daily bread' we prayed specifically for
physical healing, and included anointing with
oil at that point (James 5:14). We also prayed
about a broken relationship which had emerged
as an issue during our earlier time of listening
prayer. Interestingly, James speaks specifically
about that in his instructions on prayer for healing
(James 5:16). That led on naturally to pray for
protection in spiritual attack as a result of the
long illness the person had experienced. As we
prayed through this aspect we received several
'words of knowledge' about barriers to healing
that led us into further prayer.

This involved talking with each other, and some
crying too—as well as that cup of coffee. A relaxed
and affirming atmosphere is very important in
such prayer. Without it we can be in danger
of taking ourselves, and our part in the work
of prayer too seriously. The words of Emperor
Hirohito, the last emperor of Japan to be officially
recognised as divine, keep my sense of proportion

and perspective whenever an atmosphere of false
seriousness begins to surface in such a situation.
He said:

'You cannot imagine the extra amount of
work I had when I was a god!'

The evening ended on a note of thanksgiving for
God's evident presence with us, and affirmation
of his presence with us, and specifically with the
sick person, in the days ahead. The closing words
of Psalm 23 came to mind as we closed, namely:
'Surely goodness and love will follow me all the
days of my life, and I will dwell in the house of
the Lord for ever' (Ps 23:6).

In summary, once we have grasped this fourfold
framework we can use the Lord's Prayer as an
invitation to come into God's presence, seek the
coming of his kingdom, and go with the confidence
that he is with us.

Talk it back

What has already been said has indicated something of how the Lord's Prayer can best be
used—as headings for our own praying. In other
words, as we saw in praying back the scriptures
(Chapter Seven), we can use the principle of
'liturgical sentence and charismatic response' to
good effect here. Form and freedom are not rivals
or alternatives, but fellow-workers in the task of
prayer. Tertullian, one of the great teachers of
the early church said of the Lord's Prayer: 'Jesus

Christ our Lord has marked out for us disciples of
the New Covenant a new outline of prayer.' That
is right, it is just that, an *outline* which invites us
to fill in the details.

We can do this not only in our own praying—and
often my prayer time is simply taking fifteen to
twenty minutes to pray this prayer—but also in
praying with others. The story of the healing
prayer above is one such way. In another, very
different, and difficult, conflict situation, I was
also able to bring the group involved together
by praying our way through this fourfold framework as we addressed the issues that divided us.
Through praying it together his kingdom was
coming.

Focus it

In all the above illustrations of how I have used
this prayer, there is one important point for us
to bear in mind, namely that there is a specific
focus to the praying of the Lord's Prayer. This is
where the popular use of the prayer is, I believe,
so debilitating to its proper use.

I find the use of the phrase *'an intentional'*
helpful at this point. It is the word used by
Roman Catholics of a celebration of the mass for a
particular person or situation. So, for example, one
might hear that there will be 'an intentional mass
for Northern Ireland'. It means that there will be a
service focused around concern and prayer for the
situation in that country.

Equally, in praying the Lord's Prayer I have
found it essential to pray it in relation to some
well-defined concern. That may be as narrow a

focus as 'my life today', or as wide an issue as 'the survival of planet earth', but both give a focus and direction to the praying. What is important is that we decide what it is that we are praying for. This is part of the prayer of agreement (Matt 18:19).

This step is simply and easily done, but without it the prayer lacks direction, purpose, and thereby authenticity.

Live it

I have kept the best wine until last, for the greatest secret of the Lord's Prayer is that it was given for a threefold interlocking purpose. First it was given to teach the disciple how to pray, second to embody Jesus' whole teaching in a few memorable phrases, and third to give expression to the way of life that should arise out of such teaching. So, too, the Lord's Prayer is a prayer to be lived as well as prayed. This is why the early church gave it to candidates preparing for baptism as one of the two gospel Presentations. The Creed tells us the story of God's purposes for his world, fulfilled in the person and work of Christ, and awaiting fulfilment at the end of the age. The Lord's Prayer shows us how to join in with God's loving and life-giving purposes.

We are to walk through life living before a holy yet loving Father to whom we continually look up. We are to seek his purpose, will and kingdom in the whole of our living, trust ourselves to his provision for all we need to live a life of obedience, and celebrate the fact that we are always in his presence.

So our prayer is, finally, a going. It is a going

which involves living out of obedience to God and
in compassion for others. It enables us to break out
of any sense of a small area of life being divided off
as a spiritual compartment. Rather, in the words
of the slogan for one of the chain of motorway
service stations, it becomes 'the stop that keeps
you going'. In this way, praying the Lord's Prayer
draws us out of any dull or introverted self-focus
into the broad channel of God's mercy and love
towards his world. From prayer we rise to go in
God's name. So this prayer becomes a pattern for
our living, as we love God, work for the coming
of his kingdom, trust our needs to him, and dwell
always in his presence.

How that final stage, of dwelling in the presence
and reality of God, can happen is the subject of
the remaining two chapters. But first, a prayer
exercise on the use of the Lord's Prayer.

PRAYER EXERCISE: Meditative aid to praying the Lord's Prayer

Use this framework a number of times, until you
make it your own, then expect your use to grow
and change until it is *your* meditative aid rather
than mine. It may well take a month or two of
using this outline several times a week to reach
that point. 'Let us not become weary in doing good,
for at the proper time we will reap a harvest if we
do not give up' (Gal 6:9).

This form is a shortened one I use in the normal
course of the day. It is easily remembered, and
enables me to pray the prayer in a short space of
time—whilst waiting at the traffic lights, or for a
meeting to begin, for instance.

Our Father in heaven

Look up to the God who has made all that is, and
rejoice that he knows and cares for you.
He has given us his Spirit, so that we can call him
'Abba, Father' (Rom 8:15, Gal 4:6).
He is all-powerful yet he uses his power only in
doing good.
See yourself as part of a worldwide family that is
chosen and loved by the Father.
Rejoice that such a God actively invites us to come
before him in prayer.

Your name
Your kingdom
Your will

God's name expresses his character; meditate on
that character and its many-sidedness
– creativity, compassion, truth, holiness, justice,
  peace, mercy.
Praise God that his 'just and gentle rule' has
broken into this world, supremely in Christ.
Praise him for every way in which you are aware
of his kingdom coming in your 'world'.
Lift to him situations that cry out for the breaking
in of his kingdom.
Listen to the Spirit giving you prayer beyond your
understanding for the coming of his kingdom into
specific situations.
Be open to the gift of righteous indignation or
compassion as fuel for prayer.
Let the gulf between what is and what could/
should be, generate faith and hope for prayer.
Expect to be made eager for a new world order in
which righteousness and peace dwell.

Bring your life before God to be available to him
in his service.
Be open to his directions for your living

**Give us
Forgive us
Deliver us**

Be specific in bringing your practical needs to
God,
– especially those things you need in order to do
  the will of God.
Where you have sinned, own it, give it to God, and
receive in its place, his forgiveness.
Where you have been wronged, admit it, and
release those people from any debt to you.
– pray for God's blessing on anyone who is your
  enemy, anyone you find difficult.
Be open to God showing you any way in which you
are involved in a spiritual battle.
– ask for God's wisdom, strength, protection and
  courage to handle that situation.

**The kingdom,
The power and
The glory are yours. Amen**

Affirm the fact that God is with you wherever
you are.
Celebrate the fact that when you leave your time
of prayer, God goes with you.
Look with the eyes of faith, hope and love on the
things that you are about to turn to.

Chapter 11

Discerning the Presence of God
Seeing God in the Whole of Life

*Many of us today live in a kind of inner
apartheid. We segregate out a small corner
of pious activities and then can make no
sense of the rest of our lives.*
Richard Foster, *Prayer*, p. 179

*The sense of God is vanishing
from the earth.*
Pope John Paul II

*A culture whose people have lost all sense
of their interior lives.*
John F. Kavanaugh, *Still Following Christ in a
Consumer Society*,
(Orbis Books, Maryknoll. '91) p.3

Western society stands today in urgent need
of healing. It is a culture that has achieved
incredible technological advances, but in the process it has lost touch with its soul, with the
spiritual dimension of life, and with ultimate
meaning.

The reason for the disease we see around us,

and for the sense of moral and spiritual vacuum at the heart of our culture, lies close to the heart of our greatest successes. Our culture is brilliant at analysis. We have analysed all that is, from ourselves on the psychiatrist's couch, to the atoms that go to make up the couch, the psychiatrist and the patient. But we have lost a sense of meaning and purpose to life. We have lost touch with our humanity.

> The culture that enthrones things, products, objects as its most cherished realities, is ultimately a culture in flight from the vulnerability of the human person.
> (John F. Kavanaugh, *Still Following Christ in a Consumer Society*, [Orbis Books, Maryknoll. '91] p. 17)

The dissected frog stands (or rather lies down!) as a parable of our society. Many of us were required in our school days to dissect these poor creatures, for the cause of the advancement of science, or at any rate for the passing of exams. In the process we became much more aware of the inner contents of the frog. However, it was quite evident that this was not an advance as far as the frog was concerned. Expert though we have become in understanding its inside, the frog—if it could speak—would be crying out for someone to put it back together again.

That is the cry of our culture today—someone show us how to make life work, how to put it back together again, for we seem to have lost so much in the analysis of the parts. As T.S. Eliot put it, over sixty years ago:

Where is the Life we lost in living?
Where is the wisdom we have lost in
  knowledge?
Where is the knowledge we have lost in
  information?
The cycles of Heaven in twenty centuries
Bring us farther from God and nearer to
  the Dust.
(T.S. Eliot, *Collected Poems, 1909–1935*, p. 157)

This is why the great 'buzz word' of the New
Age movement is 'holistic': 'making whole' or
putting back together again is the desire that is
surfacing all around us. Although, as Christians,
we disagree with some of the New Age answers,
we do well to listen to the cry for wholeness and
harmony within ourselves and with all creation.

Discerning before practising

Which is where the spiritual discipline of 'practising the presence of God' comes in.

However, as I have reflected on it, I have come to
the conclusion that Christians today need to learn
a prior discipline, namely *discerning* the presence
of God. We need to do that because our culture has
initiated us into fragmented relatedness; we need
to see life as a whole. But also, if we do not first
discern God's presence in the whole of life, we will
make a fatal mistake. We will imagine that by
practising the presence of God, we are making God
present. In a culture built around manufacturing
and controlling, that would be all too easy.

But the truth is the opposite. God is already
and always present in his world. Our discipline

of practising his presence, is simply our tuning in to that Presence. This is what places discerning prior to practising. Christians in previous ages did not need to learn this discerning for they lived in a culture with a rich awareness of the supernatural and spiritual dimension.

PRAYER OF THE HEART:
Discerning God's presence.

As we look for your coming among us,
open our eyes to behold your presence,
strengthen our hands to do your will,
that the world may rejoice and give you
  praise,
Father, Son and Holy Spirit:
Blessed be God for ever!
(*Celebrating Common Prayer* [Mowbray, London '92] p. 63)

This chapter is therefore going to address our currently needed ability to discern the presence of God. Only when that is in place can we safely learn to practise the presence of the all-ready present One. Discerning God's presence is, essentially, learning to see God in the whole of life. It is living in the truth that, 'in him we live and move and have our being' (Acts 17:28). I want to highlight a number of areas of life where we can see the presence of God.

Relationships

Unless we are hermits (and therefore probably not near enough to a good Christian bookshop to obtain a copy of this book), people will play a large part in our experience of life. Life being what it is, we are likely to experience either too many, and so feel that 'our space' is being invaded; or too few, so feel that 'nobody loves me'. Whatever our relationship with others is, they play a formative part in our experience of life.

Experiencing too many is often a call from God—through the overwhelming demands—to order, or re-order our private world. God is speaking to us through people, even if only to ensure that our ultimate focus is on him. In such circumstances I have found great comfort, and not a little humour, in a passage from Mark's gospel; it reads:

> Simon and his companions went to look for him, and when they found him, they exclaimed: 'Everyone is looking for you!' Jesus replied, 'Let us go somewhere else . . .'
> (Mk 1:36–38)

Equally, too few, or too difficult a set of relationships can also be a means of encountering God, and hearing him addressing us through the pain and struggles.

However, God gives us good gifts through others too. He speaks to us often through others—Christians and non-Christians alike. Often a seemingly casual aside speaks to our heart, or touches us in some way that is the voice of God to us. Recognise the voice of God, and receive his truth—whoever and wherever it comes from. God also gives us affirmation and a sense of personal worth through others. People say good things to all of us. Sadly we brush it aside. We say 'Oh, it was nothing', when it was actually a difficult thing we did freely for

another person. Or we receive a compliment about
what we have done, or how we look, and dismiss
it by turning the conversation onto our struggle
beforehand to know how to speak or dress, or
whatever it was. Such responses may be natural,
but they are neither true, wholesome nor healthy.
They are also a form of put down to those who have
stepped out to pay us a compliment.

But God speaks to us through suffering, brokenness and pain in others too. This is the thrust of
the parable about the sheep and the goats. 'When
did we see you hungry . . .?' God addresses us in
the faces and lives of those who are the weakest.
This is why Luther advised pastors to 'spend time
with things that take life blithely, such as birds
and babies'. It is good advice: God is not just
speaking to us, he is present to us, and blessing
us through others in that moment. I think of a
couple of Downs'-syndrome young men in my last
church. They greeted people with such warmth
and joy and pleasure. I often wondered when I saw
them hugging one of our more formal members,
and me(!), 'who are the handicapped ones here?'

God also wants us to give something of himself
to others whose paths we cross—even if only
fleetingly at the check-out till. Here, I have found
that putting the blessing of God on others is a
very positive discipline. We can do that without
praying any words, just an attitude of blessing is
a prayer. Relationships are a primary channel of
God's grace in our lives.

Life

'God likes life, he invented it.' And it comes to us
by grace rather than by works or law. Our very

existence is a gift, and all the best things in life
start off free; the air we breathe, the soil we till,
the seeds we sow, come from the good hand of a
giving God.

This means that to walk in thanksgiving is to be
connected to reality. Indeed I am convinced that
if we thanked God more for what we have, such
as the pictures on our walls, or the clothes in our
wardrobes, we would need to spend less time and
money buying new ones.

Often God addresses us through life, calling us
to yield to his way and priorities in our lives, or
provoking us to faith or to action by the very
testing nature of what is happening to us. I
had been talking to a young wife and mother
recently who had been going through some very
painful struggles in her marriage, which I had
been 'strengthening her hand' to act boldly about.
After nearly a year of this pain, she said not only
that it had been the most difficult and painful year
of her life, but that God had spoken to her in and
through the pain. Then she added the striking
comment; 'For the first time in my life, I look
inside myself, and I like what I see!' God gives
even in the pain. As Neville Ward has put it:

> The process of nature, the flux of history,
> all that happens to each individual every
> twenty-four hours is a 'sum of things forever
> speaking'.
> (J. Neville Ward, *Five for Sorrow, Ten for Joy*,
> [Darton, Longman and Todd, London. '85] p. 3)

This is what the spiritual writers of old meant by
the 'blessed sacrament of the present moment'.
God comes to us in the whole of life. We discern his

presence, by listening, by hearing, by choosing, by obeying, and by returning thanks for his presence with us.

Creation

Modern life means that most of us are seriously cut off from creation, so much so that what aspects of the created order we do experience we filter out. As someone has said, in the midst of a noisy street in London or New York, most of us 'moderns' can hear a 5p coin drop, but we cannot hear the birds singing while we decide whether or not to pick it up.

We need consciously to re-connect with creation (see the poem 'Leisure' at the end of Chapter Three). We can do it by *walking in thanksgiving*. We can do it by talking thanksgiving: that is commenting on the beauty of the sky, or the sound of the bird, or whatever we are aware of.

This connects too with our ability to enjoy life, to celebrate our existence, and the existence of the whole created order. In our fragmented world we are in grave danger of having a form of spirituality that expresses that brokenness, rather than heals it. That happens when we have a narrow definition of what it is to be spiritual. It is not a compartment of life, it is a way of seeing the whole of life. That is why spirituality touches the whole of life; it is the spiritual dimension that restores wholeness, that brings integration to modern culture.

Creativity

We are made in the image of the Creator, and creativity is a whole-making activity. The forms of creativity are endless, and most of us spend most of our time in this aspect of our being. The most obvious form of creativity is work, but it is something much wider than 'paid employment'. Parents not only have the incredible privilege of bringing a new life into being (surely the greatest expression of creativity), but are also called to *create* community by 'making a family'. Creating family is one of the most vital works of our day. Creating pleasing environments, whether by art or clearing rubbish, is another vital task for today's society; as is the task of creating wealth, work, and pleasure.

It is at this point that a super-spiritual, or narrowly spiritualising, attitude to life misses so much, including the presence of God. All of us, in our places of work, and beyond them, are called—in the image of our Creator, to be creative. It is also an important aspect of discovering who we are, and in the process, discovering and discerning God's presence in the whole of life.

As we saw in the chapter on listening prayer (Chapter Eight), we make vital connection with God as we seek to listen to him about, and in, our work situations. Because of the 'dualism' so widespread in the church today, we are likely to need the help of others at this point, to discern where God is active in our work environment, and how we can be faithful to him, not just (or primarily) by evangelising those we work with, but by evangelising the whole way the work is carried out. The Hospice movement is one fine example of how Christians have 'evangelised' the care of the dying.

It is this, I suspect, that should be occupying much more of the life of the church than it currently does. We often function as Christians as though scripture said 'God so loved the church ...'. It actually says 'God so loved the *world* ...' (my italics, and his?!). We meet him there, as we listen to his leading, discern the coming of his kingdom, and commit ourselves to overcoming evil with good. Once we gain this perspective we will have much less trouble about practising the presence of God; we will be tripping over it all the time!

We are to pray over the aspects of creativity into which God has called us, in our household or family setting, our local community, our work situation, and our part in the political life of our community and country. Remember 'politics' is about the creative work of 'making city'.

The sacred canopy

We live in a secular culture—though that is rapidly changing. This culture has marginalised any sense of the sacred to the farthest corners of our community's life. It is acceptable to be 'religious' in the private realm, but public life—so the assumption goes—deals with real things, real facts, and real dependable principles. The result is that we have lost the sense of the sacred in all of creation, including the moral dimension of life. A recent report from the unlikely prophetic source of the Institute for Economic Affairs, has defined the situation well in terms of how personal, and sexual, relationships have been reduced to market forces and a consumer mentality.

The approved pattern is one of individual entrepreneurs, each free to strike a bargain

as producer of sexual gratification with any
willing consumer.
(*Families without Fatherhood* [IEA Health
and Welfare Unit, London '92] p. 66)

That is just one area of the sacred. There are many
more. The biblical view is that all of life is sacred.
This is the purpose of the ten commandments.
They are couched in negative form ('Thou shalt
not . . .'), to remind us that there are areas of
life which are 'off limits' to us. It is a major
cause for struggles in medical ethics today that
there is really no basis in a modern 'scientific
materialism' culture for denying that 'if we have
the technology, there is nothing to stop us' (such
as taking eggs from aborted foetuses). The ten
commandments put limits back into life. That is
liberating. It means that God can be seen in all
the moral issues we face, such as our life focus
(idols), use of art (images that are out of bounds),
language (taking his name in vain), the need to
stop and celebrate (sabbath), family relationships
(honouring parents), property, sexual limits, and
the right to life, as well as the one that takes us
into the New Testament dynamic of the law in the
heart (covetousness, 'which is idolatry' Col 3:5).

We live today with the fact that our abuse of
the environment has created a hole in the ozone
layer. As a result, life-threatening rays can get in
and put all existence under threat. It is a parable
of what has happened at the moral level. By
'liberating ourselves from moral constraint' we
have lost the sacred canopy which we need to
protect us from the harmful effect of the creature
playing God.

The sacred canopy not only sets limits, but

it establishes shalom (peace, harmony, balance).
It establishes the framework within which connectedness between men and women, humanity and creation, people and property, creatures
and Creator can work. As we see moral issues
around us, we will find God, and his kingdom
at work drawing attention to connectedness and
balance—the mobile of the cosmos.

Once we see this, we can begin to sense the
presence of God, brooding and grieving (Gen 1:2;
Rom 8:22, 23, 26—the threefold groaning), over
the travail of contemporary moral dilemmas, and
the 'valueless' world into which we are educating
the next generation. The newspapers and TV and
radio news are as good a way of seeking to *see* the
sacred canopy as any. Our world stands in urgent
need of re-sacralising. We assist that missionary
endeavour every time we discern the presence of
God in the moral dilemmas we face as individuals,
as families, communities, or as a society.

Walking in communion

The sacrament of communion is built around two
themes. The first is that of thanksgiving. It is a
service of thanksgiving (that is what the Greek
work 'eucharist' means) from beginning to end.
The prayer exercise which follows is designed to
strengthen our ability to walk through the whole
of life with an attitude, and in the practice, of
thanksgiving. It is the bridge between discerning
and practising the presence of God.

The other theme of communion is what is called
the 'fourfold action'. This refers to the four things

that Jesus did when he instituted communion. He took, blessed, broke and gave the elements to his disciples. The exercise which follows is built around that fourfold action. Henri Nouwen's little book, *Life of the Beloved* (Hodder & Stoughton, London '92) uses this as the basis for 'spiritual living in a secular world'. As we make ourselves at home in this structure, we will find that we are not only discerning God's presence more readily in the whole of life, but also that we are more immediately at home when we come to receive communion at church.

PRAYER EXERCISE: Practising communion

Review the last hour, day, or week, and
– thank God that he is with you now.
Then give thanks for the good gifts of life
– for physical and mental health which we take so much for granted: receive them now ('hands up') as gifts given new each day.
– for the people in your life without whom you would feel lost or less.
– for the creation around you (for example, within one hundred yards).
– for the areas of creativity in which you are participating: do not focus on the failures; enjoy the gift and opportunity at this point.
– for the moral dimension that is gift to your life.

Now picture Jesus coming to you in this setting in your life.

Taking
He knows us, cares about us, takes us in his arms,
calls us by name.
In him we belong: we have security, meaning,
purpose.
We are not alone in the universe.
We are friends of the Creator.
Surrender to a Love that is affirming and life-
giving.

Blessing
You have learned to put the blessing of God on
others, now put it on yourself.
Hear God speaking the Aaronic blessing over
you.
See his eye upon you in affirming love.
Be open, in listening prayer, to particular words
of affirmation God may give you now.
– note them down, build them into the liturgy of
   your heart.

Breaking
Trust him with those areas of pain, frustration,
and creatureliness with which you struggle at
present.
Like the clay, dare to yield to his reshaping
– remember it is *his* re-shaping, not the manipu-
   lation or control of others, that we yield to.
Let the process of Cross-and-Resurrection do its
enriching work in you.

Giving
See God taking you as a *gift* that he is giving to
those around.
See him giving you to your family/household,
work, community, friends.

Be open to how he desires that gift to be given,
- be aware of any promptings of the Spirit about
  ways in which he is calling you to give yourself
  to others.

Conclude by returning to thanksgiving
- for life, for being part of God's purposes in
  human history, for God himself.

Chapter 12

Practising the Presence of God
Encountering God in the Whole of Life

*In understanding the true nature of prayer,
it is a mistake to draw too rigidly the
frontier between prayer and life.*
Michael Ramsey, *Be Still and Know* (Collins,
Fount Paperbacks, London. '82) p. 12

*Life is shaped, moment by moment, through
an awareness of the 'Significant Other'
who gives meaning to our reality.
Prayer in whatever form is the means to
maintaining this awareness.*
Jack Dominian, *Cycles of Affirmation* (Darton,
Longman and Todd, London. '75) p. 122

Now we have seen how God is present and active in his world, we can start to discover his presence, and act on the truth of it, even when we do not have conscious evidence of it. We are ready to tackle the art of 'practising the presence'. But what is it?

What it is not, and the last chapter sought to establish this, is our making God present in a

way which, without our efforts, he would not be.
We are creatures of the Creator of all that is. So
practising the presence is becoming in touch with
what is, not creating what is not.

This practice can be described in a number of
ways. One such way is to say that practising
the presence of God is *living out the two great
commandments*, to love God and love others, as
ourselves. It is to live life within the interlocking pattern of love—for God, others and the
self.

Another way of describing practising the presence is that it is *living in the gospel*, celebrating
the good news that God is with us, and that he
has promised to be with us 'to the close of the age'.
It is discovering the reality of the commandment
to 'remain in me' (Jn 15:1–17) and so 'bear much
fruit'.

Equally, it is *living as a child of God* (Lk
18:15–17 with Lk 8:19–21), able to enjoy the
present moment, able to look up in wonder and
live fully in the present moment, being in touch
with ourselves and the surrounding community,
and to centre our living upon God himself. That
includes the capacity to celebrate.

Supremely it is *the enjoyment of God himself*,
as the Westminster catechism puts it, 'our chief
end is to glorify God and to enjoy him for ever'.
However, let me immediately qualify this by saying that this is not some artificial or hothouse
spirituality. Indeed its heart is the opposite—a
capacity to dance, to play, and to be human. It
is the capacity not only to enjoy and know the
presence of God, it is to receive and enjoy his
gifts. A child at Christmas saying 'thank you'
to its parents for the wrapped present, shows

its appreciation by unwrapping the present and
enjoying it. So too for us, the enjoyment of relationship with God includes the ability to enjoy his
gifts of creation, humanity, friends and life itself.
As James Philip puts it:

> The deepest word that can be spoken about
> sanctification is that it is a progress towards
> humanity. Salvation is, essentially consid-
> ered, the restoration of humanity to man.
> This is why the slightly inhuman, not to
> say unnatural, streak in some forms and
> expressions of sanctification is so far removed
> from the true work of grace in the soul.
>
> The greatest saints of God have been char-
> acterised, not by haloes and an atmosphere
> of distant unapproachability, but by their
> humanity. They have been intensely human
> and lovable people with a twinkle in their
> eyes.
>
> (James Philip, *Christian Maturity*,
> [IVF, London. '64] p. 70)

To practise the presence of God is to re-discover
connectedness, with ourselves, with the whole of
life, and with God. An over-spiritualising of it into
'conscious awareness of God' is actually to partake
of the brokenness of our present culture which is
disconnected, and disintegrated. Practising the
presence of God involves both enjoying God as
the supreme goal of all that is, but also enjoying
all that he has given us: it is to celebrate the reality
and goodness of the Creator and the creation. Just
as you do not do an artist the greatest honour by
always looking at him and never at his paintings,
so we do not fully enjoy God unless we develop the

capacity to enjoy all that is. As C.S. Lewis put it, so succinctly, 'To experience the tiny theophany (a moment or means of God revealing himself) is to adore.' (*Prayer: Letters to Malcolm*, p. 91.) To enter into the playing of a child, the beauty of sun on autumn leaves, or an understanding look from a friend is to be alive to God in his universe.

For this reason, the particular skill that I believe we need to recapture today is this ability to rediscover connectedness or integration, and see all life as in God, and God touching us in the whole of life.

An important distinction

Before we move on to consider practical steps that we can take to live before God in the whole of life, I want to make an important distinction which Leanne Payne makes in her book *The Healing Presence*. It is that there is a difference between the *practice* of the presence and the *sense* of the presence of God. The *practice* is our part, part of our spiritual discipline: the *sense* of God's presence is his gift to give when and how he chooses. We will not always *sense* God's presence. Indeed if we did there would be no ground for faith—it would all be by sight. However, as we learn to practise God's presence we will experience moments of great closeness to, and enjoyment of, God. It is right to savour and enjoy such moments, but not make the experience greater than the One experienced. C.S. Lewis's book, *Surprised by Joy*, is the testimony of someone who missed God for many years because he sought the experience of joy rather than the Source of joy.

Into action

All the previous chapters have ended with a
'prayer exercise'. This one, because of its subject,
needs to be different. What now follows is the
'exercise' part of the chapter. As such it contains
a whole series of 'exercises' which are to be done
not in the times we withdraw to prayer, but in
the midst of life. It is important not to attempt
to become familiar with all of them at the same
time. That would be a recipe for spiritual exhaus-
tion. My encouragement, rather, is to take one of
them at a time—for a month or two—and develop
proficiency in it; making it, as we have seen in
other aspects of the prayer life, part of how *we*
pray. It is good to note in one's prayer journal
what the focus will be, and any ways in which you
sense that progress is being made. If you can work
with someone else—a prayer partner, or as part of
the life and work of a home group—so much the
better.

Do not be discouraged by seeming failures and
by 'nothing happening'. If we exercise the discipline of practising God's presence, he will give
the gift of awareness and awe in his timing and
in his ways. And we had better be prepared for
God's surprises, his tap on our shoulder to look
in the opposite direction from the one we were
looking in, for us to see him. This is what Jesus
was doing with Peter when he told him to cast the
net on the 'other side'. It was what God was doing
with a friend of mine who, when ill, naturally
sought prayer for healing from those gifted in that
work—only to discover that the healing actually
came when he was drinking a pint of beer. God
gives himself through the whole of creation. He

is the God of surprises. So let's get on with the
joyful work of practising his presence.

Rhythms and routines

We are creatures of habit, and that is a good thing,
but it also suggests how we should handle our
praying; by tying it in with the regular patterns of
our living. The Celtic Christians were very good at
this, and had prayers for lighting fires, prayers for
milking cows, and prayers—it seems—for every
eventuality.

Few of us light fires, other than by the flick of
a switch, and even fewer of us today milk cows!
But we do have routines. Walking to work, driving
to work, shaving, ironing, cleaning the car, and
a thousand-and-one other regular chores. Chores
which do not occupy the whole of our minds. It is
good to make connection between such routines
and the discipline of 'calling on the name of the
Lord'. Maybe there is a time of the day that you
can fix in your mind 'I will always pray at . . .'; or
maybe there is a roundabout on your way to work
that you can make your 'prayer roundabout'.

Where I last worked I walked to my office. It was
a five-minute walk, and I decided to commit myself
to praying whilst doing that walk—on some occasions four times a day—there and back. At first I
often forgot: to be honest, the norm was to forget,
the exception was to pray! However, I stuck at it,
and found I was praying more often. Rather than
berate myself for not praying, whenever I noticed
that I was not doing so, I used it to prompt me to
turn to prayer. Within a year I was praying for a

part of the walk, even if only the last few paces.
Then I discovered a fascinating thing. Initially I
had caught myself not praying, and so started to
pray. After eighteen months (yes, good habits do
take time to grow) I realised that I was sometimes
'catching myself praying'. I had got into prayer
without being aware of consciously doing so. Be
encouraged, addiction to prayer can become habit
forming!

Liturgy of the heart

I have looked at this in an earlier chapter, but I
want to return to it at this point since, it is—in my
experience—very closely related to the first way of
practising God's presence. Gerard Hughes says:

> Christian tradition recognises that it is dif-
> ficult for busy and active people to be still,
> and that is why many traditional methods
> of prayer are very repetitive, the repetition
> being designed to still the mind.
> (Gerard Hughes, *God of Surprises*, p. 45)

This is classically true of what is known as the
'Jesus prayer', which is

> Lord Jesus Christ, Son of God, have mercy
> upon me, a sinner.

The art is in learning to write the truth on our
hearts so that it becomes part of us. I remember
one occasion when I had been speaking. I felt
particularly unhappy about both 'it' (the talk),
and myself. I sat down and 'called on the name of

the Lord', slowly repeating this Jesus prayer. My conscious mind was hardly engaged, but I prayed this prayer perhaps twenty or thirty times. My 'attitude' was one of saying it as a cry to God; expressing a sense of failure and despair. Within five minutes I had such a strong sense of the love of God around me that I knew I was 'accepted in the Beloved'. It did not make any difference to my assessment of the talk, but it certainly made a difference to me, my view of life, and my experience of God.

I have developed, over the years, various 'shaving liturgies'. At this point I am probably one up on our Celtic forbears because that is possibly one thing they did not have a prayer for! One such prayer has been:

I am chosen in your grace, accepted in your love, made complete in Christ.

Notice that this is in the form of affirmation of truth, rather than request for anything. We have explored this dimension earlier.

PRAYER OF THE HEART:
A Celtic prayer of connectedness.

Bless to us, O God,
The sun that is above us,
The earth that is beneath us,
The friends who are around us,
Your image deep within us,
The day which is before us. Amen.

(as a 'night prayer', replace 'moon' for 'sun', and 'rest' for 'day')

Emotions and the inner dialogue

Our emotional life is a vast, untapped resource for prayer and for practising the presence of God. It has been given to us to energise us for life. Anger motivates us to 'do something about the situation', tenderness makes us gentle with a suffering person or situation, fear focuses our need to find a way through—or out.

All of our emotions can be 'energy for life', simply by 'turning the inner dialogue up to God'. All of us spend much of our time having a dialogue with ourselves. If we could but hear it, it is often not very complimentary to ourselves—except when insecurity fuels pride and we become 'grandiose' and see ourselves as God's answer to everyone's prayer. One ready source of engaging with God is to turn that inner dialogue up to God. It will very often help us to see the situation or issue in a different light. It will open us up to new, and more creative solutions than our instinct to 'shoot the lot of them'!

PRAYER PRINCIPLE SEVEN
EMOTIONAL ENERGY IS FUEL
FOR PRAYER
Many of us do not often 'feel like praying'.
But we do feel many other things.
We feel sad, angry, relieved, joyful, anxious,
puzzled. To pray, all we need to do is harness
that emotional energy as fuel that lifts our
prayers, and ourselves, to God.

Turning the inner dialogue up to God involves sharing with him our actual thoughts and feelings, listening to the underlying attitudes to ourselves and others (whether of pride, or its cousin, self-pity), and listening to God's answer to what is going on within. Much of the Psalms is the account of the Psalmist's inner dialogue coming out—and going up to God. It is a vital way of staying connected to God.

Listening in life

Francis MacNutt, in his book *Healing*, says that we should learn to listen to people with one ear, whilst turning the other one to listen to God for his will and word in the situation. That is how we are to live in the whole of life—listening to God. As we do so, we walk in, and into, his presence. By contrast, Paul Tournier says:

> Listen to all the conversations of the world, those between couples and those between nations, and you will find that they are for the most part dialogues of the deaf.

The Christian is called to listen. We saw this in the chapter on listening prayer, but it is more than an agenda for prayer, it is a way of life. It involves listening to others, to body language, to the hidden agenda, to the strong emotions that often run just below the surface of many a clinically detached conversation.

It also involves listening to our own emotions, as for example Jesus did in Gethsemane. The first thing he did was to tell the Father how he felt. Only then could he discover God's will. Listening to our own emotions connects us with ourselves. Connection with God comes more easily after that.

We listen to God's call when it comes to us
through the challenge of circumstances we are
placed in. Prayer can be a thought, an attitude,
rather than a verbal action. In that thought we
recognise the sacredness of all life, and seek to
make a response that pleases God.

In, and beyond, all these ways, we are to listen
to God; for to be a Christian is to live out of
response to the call of God in the whole of our
living. Just as Jesus 'only did what he saw the
Father doing' (Jn 5:19), so we are to stay in tune
with God. Paul's advice to the Colossians was to
'let the peace of Christ rule in your hearts' (Col
3:15); 'ruling' means 'acting as arbitrator'. We
are, as the Quakers say, to 'follow our peace'. I
have found, on a number of occasions, where I have
had to make decisions with limited information (a
permanent human state as I now see it), I have
sought to decide by choosing what I can best live
with if I am proved wrong by subsequent events.

Many other ways

Most, if not all, of what has been said in this
book can be practised, not only in specific times
of prayer, but as attitudes to life, and ways of
practising the presence of God. So, for example,
what we have just been considering is simply
the moment by moment practice of the *listening
prayer* which we looked at in Chapter Eight.

Beholding the throne can be done in a moment
by carrying in our hearts the words 'Our Father'.
It is not necessary to say them, just to see them;
or rather, like icons, to see through them to the
truth and reality and glory of God to which they

make a way open. Equally, the exercises taught so far, all have 'practising the presence' applications. Waiting in a bus queue at the end of an afternoon shopping, or after a busy day at the office, is a natural time to practise the *'letting go before God'* exercise. You do not need to sit down to do it, but it helps to let your hands hang down so you can sense your trials and strains pouring out of your fingers. Hands turned forwards can be expressive of waiting to receive gifts of life.

The bus queue is also a good time to put *the blessing of God* on people; joy to the glum, friends for the lonely, peace for the restless, faith for the self-confident, can all be 'put' on those around us.

Being of a mischievous, and economical, nature I have found a way—since becoming an occasional commuter on the London Underground—of reading other peoples' newspapers with a good conscience. I simply look for headlines which I can turn into *prayers of lament*, or *prayers of blessing*. It makes a game of prayer, but then salvation is, in part, restoration of our ability, and permission, to play in the universe—before the Father.

Summary

I began, way back in the Introduction, by explaining why someone, called to help the church evangelise, should get 'distracted' into writing a book on prayer. It is appropriate therefore, as I bring this section, on *going* as a result of meeting God in prayer, to a close to make the connection between prayer and evangelism.

The mystics of medieval times said that evangelism is the sharing of the fruits of contemplation. And so it is. The only authentic good news we have is the good news of our present encounter with God. The more widely that stream flows, overflowing the narrow channels of intercession, fellowship, and public acts of worship, to irrigate the whole of life, the more complete and integrated we will be, and the more will be multiplied the points of connection with a world that is hungry for contact with Ultimate Reality. Which is why, making contact with the whole of life, and being in touch with ourselves, others, life, creation and God are such evangelistic endeavours. If we could but live that way we would find many asking us for 'a reason for the hope that is in us' (1 Pet 3:15), for the knowledge of God does bring hope, and that is a scarce commodity in today's culture.

I ended the Introduction with the story of Abba Joseph speaking about being 'all flame'. So now I end on the same note, by recounting the comment made of St Francis, which surely expresses the desire of our hearts, for . . .

> It was said of St Francis that he 'seemed not so much a man praying as prayer itself made man.'
>
> (Richard Foster, *Prayer*, p. 125)

God grant that we may enter into such fullness of life, as God has made possible for all, in Christ. May the glory be all his, as the blessing will assuredly be all ours, and those whose lives are touched by God's life in us, as we discover prayer as a deep and joyful affair of our heart.

Postscript

Implementing Practicalities

> *Training in prayer should be*
> *the main preoccupation and service*
> *given by bishops and clergy*
> *to the adult members of the church.*
> Gerard Hughes, *God of Surprises*, p. 22

> *Too little prayer is an expression of unbelief*
> *in God's love and care;*
> *so is too much.*
> Richard Lovelace, *Dynamics of Spiritual Life*
> (Paternoster Press, Exeter: '79) p. 160

There are one or two things I want to say by way of conclusion concerning the practice of prayer. I have two things to say to individuals, one is a health warning about too much prayer, and the other is about the making and use of a prayer journal. Then I want to make some suggestions about now the material in this book can help in corporate prayer, and how corporate prayer can strengthen personal prayer. This dimension of 'fellowship in prayer' covers the application of this material in home groups and whole churches.

Too much prayer can damage your spiritual health!

It may seem a strange way to end a book on prayer, by warning of the dangers of too much prayer, but it is necessary. And it is not just too much prayer that is the danger. The harm comes from taking ourselves too seriously, and by acting out of (often unconscious) pride, which imagines that prayer is simply 'something I do'. Prayer is a partnership. It should not take us long to work out who is the senior partner.

Our problem stems from living in a man-centred technological society addicted to taking control. When archaeologists come to dig up the remains of twentieth-century Western civilisation in a few thousand years time, they need to dig up a remote control unit—it is the primary artefact of our culture. Control without effort, without contact. Take that mentality into prayer, and we will be in for trouble, for to assume that our prayer life is primarily dependent on us is what will seriously damage our knowledge of God.

We had better remember that we can sin by the way we pray (remember the parable of the Pharisee and the publican). The sin I have in mind is that of thinking that prayer all depends on us and our effort. Remember, sin has been defined as our determination to manage by ourselves. All prayer that stems from trying too hard, taking ourselves too seriously, and any driven-ness is unhealthy prayer.

From beginning to end we are sustained by God and his grace. We may be able to exist without other people, but we can no more exist without God than a television picture can exist without electricity. It is God who is the primary agent in sustaining our prayer life, which is why opening up to God is a vital first step into prayer. He is the one who draws our heart after him. He is the one who keeps us growing in prayer.

God as initiator of our praying

We do well to remember the other side of the whole thrust of this book. Looking back we can see all the truths about prayer which we have explored, *from God's side. It is the greater truth.*

God has encountered us. Our encounter is a response to his initiative. 'Discipleship is first and foremost a response to an invitation' (Henri Nouwen in his foreword to *We Drink From our Own Wells,* by Gustav Gutierrez).

God beholds us. He never forgets us (Is 49:15). He will never leave or forsake us (Jos 1:5, Heb 13:5). Our names are written on the palms of his hands (Is 49:16).

God's word takes hold of us. We came to faith because God spoke his life-giving word into our lives. We continue because he continues to do so. His Word 'will not return to me empty, but will accomplish what I desire and achieve the purpose for which I sent it' (Is 55:11). Whether God's Word comes to us as hammer (Jer 23:29) or honey (Ps 19:10), it is the power of God and will do its work in us.

God is always listening to us. His ear is attentive to the cry of his people, he knows their suffering and he comes down to deliver them (Ex 3:7–8).

God intercedes through us. It is the Spirit who prays through us. It is God who prays in and

through us. He gives us the gift of intercession.
We do not have to work it up. It is the Spirit
who enables us to cry '*Abba*, Father' (Rom 8:15),
the Spirit who alone enables us to say 'Jesus is
Lord' (1 Cor 12:3), and the Spirit who breathes
life, energy and often the very words themselves,
into our formless, or half-formed, prayers (Rom
8:26–27).

He practises his presence in us. He took the initiative in the incarnation to be Emmanuel—God-
with-us. He gave us the Holy Spirit to be with us
always. Every day is Christmas Day—Christ born
in us. Every day is Easter Day, Christ risen among
us. Every day is a Pentecost; the Spirit poured out
upon us. All we need is buckets of faith big enough
to contain such generous outpourings.

We do well to remember these things when we
have any wrong sense of achieving in prayer. We
also need to hold onto these things when we
are too ill or weak to pray. Another is with us.
Another is in us. It is all done by grace. As
Richard Lovelace puts it when he eschews the
use of 'spiritual ladders' as a way of instruction
in prayer:

> Ladders are always intimidating, and it is
> my suspicion that Christians should always
> assume that they start each day at the top of
> the ladder in contact with God and renew this
> assumption whenever they appear to have
> slipped a rung.
> (Richard Lovelace, *Dynamics of Spiritual Life*
> [Paternoster Press, Exeter: '79] p. 19)

Whenever we take ourselves too seriously, or
become over-anxious about our effort in prayer,

we would be well advised to meditate our way
through the italicised list of this section, and
recover perspective—for the glory of God, and
the good of our own souls.

Creating a prayer journal

Throughout this book, have attempted to be practical. I have not sought to write a book which simply
leaves people better informed about prayer. My
desire has been to leave the reader better formed
in prayer. For this reason I want to add some
comments about the practical details of how to
develop both personal prayer and corporate prayer
through the use of this book.

As far as the aspect of personal prayer is concerned, the whole book has been geared to that
goal. There are plenty of exercises to keep an
active pray-er going for years. My encouragement
is to use the book in that way. Having read this far,
the best way to use it is to keep it near wherever
you usually pray, and to dip into it, developing
one aspect of your seeing, knowing and going as
appropriate. Keep at it long enough, through that
discipline of what C.S. Lewis called 'counting the
steps', until you have made it your own and it has
become part of how you pray.

However, there is one aspect of personal prayer
that I have hinted at, but not pulled together in
a co-ordinated way so far, and I want to add a
few practical suggestions about it. It concerns the
matter of creating and using a prayer journal.

My 'prayer journal' is scattered around the
room in which I normally pray, with icons on

the walls, a pottery chalice and patten on the
sideboard, a tape recorder to hand, and my journal
in a spiral 'reporters notebook' on the table beside
the chair in which I sit. I say this to reassure the
less than totally organised people that you can
pray even if you are like that!

However, it could be better organised. It would
be if I did not have the luxury of my own study.
Here is how I would set about such an organisation.

I would use a smallish (say A5 paper) ring binder
with three major dividers in it. Yes, you have
guessed, the divisions would be seeing, knowing
and going.

Seeing

In the *seeing section* I would paste in icons that
spoke to me, as well as other pictures, and the
words of hymns that found an echo in my experience and approach to God. My own, or other
people's prayers of adoration would find a home
here. As would anything else which aided me in
my seeing of God.

Knowing

The *knowing section* would almost certainly be
the longest one. This is the value of a loose-leaf
approach as you can make each section just as
long, or short, as is appropriate. In this part of
the journal I would have a number of different
elements. Ideally they might be sub-divided from
each other; in reality they get jumbled up in my
journal simply according to the date on which it
came to me. I actually find that filing by date

is one of the best ways of filing as I can easily
forget which heading I put something under, but
I usually have a fair instinct for *when* I thought
or wrote that particular matter. All too easily, for
me, filing systems lapse into 'a convenient way of
losing things alphabetically'!

Nevertheless, here are the various elements
in my prayer journal. First are prayers. Among
these are set prayers which I use regularly. For
example, one of my favourites is the collect from
the Alternative Services Book (1980), which I
use in connection with renewing my awareness
of being called by Love (see p.75).

I also write down *some* of my own prayers in my
journal. Which ones? Well, the ones that I sense
'resonate' with my life, are God-given prayers,
and need to be prayed repeatedly until they are
part of the liturgy of my heart. They will often
take the form of an affirmation, rather than a
request. One such prayer I have used recently, also
in connection with being called into being, is:

> The God of the universe,
> celebrates my existence. Alleluia

So any prayer that I sense should become part
of me, I write down—usually with an asterisk
beside it. I do the latter because I also write
other prayers which are dealing with an important
matter *today* but which I do not think will be part
of a continuing prayer. Leanne Payne quotes a
person who said 'How can I know what I think
until I hear what I say', which I find very true for
my prayer life. Writing it down is important in the
process of 'getting it out'. Which is also why I pray
out loud—though not loudly!

In this section on *knowing* I also record what I sense God has been saying to me. This may take the form of verses from scripture, or some way in which my praying back of the scriptures has touched me deeply. Here also I record the words that have come to me as I have sought to practise listening prayer. I write down all that comes; and then, reviewing it later, I put an asterisk against any that seem to be of abiding importance.

I also record dreams that are saying something important, and the reflections on them that emerge from praying them back to God.

Going

The final part of a prayer journal is the going section. Here I would have a page for my intercessions list(s), although I kept this simple because I have spent too much of my Christian life laying unreasonable burdens for prayer on myself. I found great liberation through the comment of Richard Lovelace quoted in Chapter Nine ('Intercession').

This section would also include pictures which speak to me of our mission in prayer and in life. A picture of pollution to aid my intercession for the care of the environment, and a picture from Bosnia, Somalia, or Northern Ireland to aid the focus of my prayer for those troubled environments.

I would also have a page with a list of major events coming up in the next few months, over which I could be praying.

Here, also, is where I would put those prayers which assist my practising the presence of God, including, for example, the one from *Celebrating Common Prayer*, found on p.164.

Lest this all sounds too holy and disciplined to
be true, let me add that I do not pick up my prayer
journal every day (even every week). There are
seasons where I use it daily, and seasons when
it has time off for a few weeks. It is an aid, not
a duty.

Implementing in a prayer or home group

Ever since Jesus taught his disciples to pray 'Our
Father . . .', Christians have discovered how much
stronger their prayer life can be if it is a corporate
experience. That is not to suggest that corporate
prayer is a substitute for private prayer. However,
I do believe that corporate prayer is the foundation
for private prayer. It roots us in a community,
gives us some corporate disciplines, and enriches
our prayer through exposure to the prayers of
others.

I commend, therefore, the idea of using this book
as a basis for corporate prayer in a home group. It
would simply be a matter of the group agreeing
to do so. Each person would need a copy of the
book, and different sections of the material could
be worked on from time to time. Maybe once or
twice a month half an hour could be given over to
doing one of the exercises.

On another occasion an evening could be spend
talking over, and then practising, a whole chapter.
It would be best if everyone read the chapter—
ideally a week or more in advance of the meeting—and then sought to practise the particular
content. At the meeting, after a brief summary of

the chapter by someone, people could share joys
and sorrows, seeming successes and failures with
each other. Remember, sharing sorrows, struggles
and frustrations, is as great a blessing as sharing
glorious successes; for it keeps the conversation
real, rather than ideal, and draws out of others
insights and care for the person who has opened
their heart.

It would be important for the evening to end
with the practice of the material, in the light of
the corporate reflections and experiences. In this
way the personal discipline of prayer would be
greatly strengthened and affirmed, and the book
might become the group's 'prayer book' for a few
years. There might be seasons when several weeks
are devoted to working on this material, and other
times when a half-hour practice once or twice a
month was sufficient, to sustain mutual support
and growth in prayer.

Implementing in the church

My final word is to church leaders and clergy who
have the opportunity to help the whole church
bring about the renewal of personal prayer. My
conviction is that we often preach on prayer,
but much less often, see significant movement
or increase in the practice of it.

Our problem is that we handle the preaching ministry in isolation from the total training
environment of the church. It simply does not
work if treated like that. We need rather to
see that there is a *preaching-teaching-training-
talking-continuum* at work in the church. By this

I mean that when we discern that God is wanting something to be 'birthed' in the church, then the whole life of the church needs to be geared to that end.

So, for example, properly to stand a chance of renewing personal prayer in the life of a church one would be best advised to take a whole series of steps. Here is a possible programme. There is nothing fixed about it, each local church would need to adapt the ideas. The important point is that every area of the life of the church needs to be incorporated if the church is to be an effective teaching environment. Your situation may call for a very different approach in one or more of these elements. That is fine. The vital thing is that *some* connection with the renewal of personal prayer should be made across the board. It is this lack of the wholeness, and so wholesomeness, of the teaching environment that causes isolated sermon series to be seemingly impotent to bring about change. The horse is not connected to the carriage. The engine of truth is not in gear with the wheels of change.

Here then is a suggested strategy for renewing personal prayer in the life of a whole church.

It would be good to gain as wide *agreement* as possible that this was the right aim, and the necessary priority—maybe over the period of a whole year. Indeed, a church council that agreed to such an emphasis, could usefully set up a small '*monitoring* group' that could find out the extent of people's prayer life by use of a sensitive (maybe anonymous) questionnaire at the beginning of this exercise, and then repeat the questionnaire a year later. Monitoring can also be done at more anecdotal level by asking people how they are 'getting on with all this prayer stuff the Vicar is going on about'!

Such a plan does not mean that nothing else would be taught or done—that could result in overkill—but rather that this would be the underlying theme, and one to which, after each Festival, the church returned.

It might well be good to start with a pump-priming *teaching weekend* in which the *seeing, knowing, going* framework was outlined and—as far as possible—practised.

Preaching, could valuably pick up, and illustrate the theme of prayer, for example by a series of sermons on encounters with God, or the Lord's Prayer, or the prayers of scripture, or through exposition of some devotional psalms. In this way the attention of the church can be brought back to the theme regularly.

Home groups could be encouraged to use the material as outlined in the previous section.

Obviously the aim is that *individuals* practise this material. To aid this, in addition to what is already suggested, it would be good for individuals who have experienced God through a renewed prayer life, to be invited to share the same with the whole congregation. It would also be valuable for the subject to be on the agenda of *personal conversations* as part of pastoral care. Paul clearly practised this type of ministry, when he says to the Ephesian church leaders, at the end of his ministry with them, 'You know that I have not hesitated to preach anything that would be helpful to you but have taught you publicly and from house to house' (Acts 20:20).

However, when all the above has been done, there is one missing ingredient, which is of tremendous

importance. It is all part of implementing in the local
church, and is of sufficient importance to deserve a
section of its own.

Implementing in public worship

The church's coming together involves a whole
number of symbolic actions (whether it is officially
a 'liturgical church' or not) which give identity,
meaning, and significance to the whole group
and to the individuals in it. That is why people
come, to belong to a group with this particular
set of interests, concerns and values in common.
Public worship therefore provides a vital time
for teaching and training by the whole way it is
conducted.

If our goal is to renew personal prayer, then the
more that what we are encouraging individuals
to do on their own is supported and reinforced
when we come together (both in home groups,
committee meetings and teams) but especially in
the corporate acts of community making which is
what Sunday worship is, the greater will be the
effect.

So how do we set about communicating about
personal prayer through public acts of worship,
apart from preaching? Basically by building it into
every aspect of the worship. So, for example, the
opening part of the worship could be consciously
related to our seeing of God. It might be appropriate to have a verse from a hymn on the duplicated
notices, or on the overhead projector, and invite
people to focus on God in preparation for the
service. Many churches today are a hubbub of

noise before the service. One can either stand up
and ask people to be quiet and give them a focus
to their *seeing* five minutes before the service, or
do it as the first five minutes of the worship (after
giving a welcome and any notices).

The *confession* should tie in with the material
on 'Good Grief' and should carefully model how to
make confession.

Readings from scripture can be followed by 60
to 90 seconds of silence between the end of the
reading and the use of the response 'This is the
word of the Lord: thanks be to God'. If you are
going to do this then people need to be prepared
for it—not least if they are used to following the
passage in the church Bibles, since they will all
shut their books when they are meant to be meditating on the text!

The *intercessions* are obviously of vital importance in modelling the 'how' of personal prayer.
Material from the relevant chapter could be picked
up and used in leading the intercessions. A useful
monitoring job is for someone to be set aside to
record the amount of time actually allocated to
silence. The practice is so widespread of those
leading in prayer saying 'Let us in silence pray
for . . .' and then leaving no time for silence—or
often, in my experience, just about enough for me
to register that I can dare to let go and pray myself,
but not enough time to do so!

Again, the *Lord's Prayer* is something that
should play a vital part in personal and corporate
prayer. If, as the material on the subject in this
book argues, we think that the Lord's Prayer needs
to be focused, then it is vital that those leading
in worship do actually do so before leading the
church into the use of it. Using a sung form

can also enhance its value; as can the use of it as headings for a whole section of intercession. When we do that we are 'modelling' prayer for each individual.

This is not a complete list of implementing the renewal of personal prayer in public worship, but I hope it is sufficient to enable those who conduct public worship to see how crucial what we do together on Sunday is to the shaping and strengthening of what we do in private during the week. Equally it can seriously undermine it if the connection is not properly made. My conviction, borne of experience, is that training in prayer (or any other matter) is not to be measured in terms of:

personal prayer + home group prayer + preaching + practice in Sunday services
but rather by the equation:
personal prayer × home group prayer × preaching × practice in Sunday services

If we could but get our act together, in allowing the work of renewing personal prayer to shape the renewal of corporate prayer, and—at the same time—allow the practice of corporate prayer to reinforce the renewal of private prayer, we might see something very significant happening in the life of the church today. Which brings me back to the starting point of my Introduction about why an 'officer for evangelism' is writing about prayer. It is my conviction that the only authentic good news we have to proclaim is that which has touched our heart in the intimacy of prayer. As John Talbot puts it:

We cannot give what we do not have, we
cannot evangelise others until God has evangelised us.

(John Michael Talbot *Blessings:*
Reflections on the Beatitudes, p. 18)

To conclude. The prayer exercise that awaits us is
the total work of personal prayer, and in so far as
we have responsibility for it, the renewal of the
prayer life of the home group, or local church
for which we have responsibility. We can know
that any steps in that work delight the heart
of the God who delights in us. Such work is
life-giving participation in God's purposes for his
whole creation. May we find joy in knowing that
we are part of that great work.